T0115088

LAST CHANCE MILE

The Reinvention of an
American Community

ROD KACKLEY

abbott press®
A DIVISION OF WRITER'S DIGEST

Last Chance Mile
The Reinvention of an American Community

ISBN: 978-1-4582-0448-6 (sc)
ISBN: 978-1-4582-0449-3 (e)
ISBN: 978-1-4582-0450-9 (hc)

Library of Congress Control Number: 2012910956

Abbott Press books may be ordered through booksellers or by contacting:

Abbott Press
1663 Liberty Drive
Bloomington, IN 47403
www.abbottpress.com
Phone: 1-866-697-5310

Printed in the United States of America

Abbott Press rev. date: 08/29/12

To everyone on Medical Mile and in the city of Grand Rapids working on the reinvention of this American community, with special thanks to my family, Erin, Ben and Krystal; along with Jim Cox, and Jana Doubrava who have really helped with this work.

"It always seems impossible until it's done."
Nelson Mandela

Contents

INTRODUCTION

THERE ISN'T A CITY in Michigan or many in the United States that are not trying to reinvent themselves following the Great Recession. *Last Chance Mile: The Reinvention of an American Community* tells the story of Grand Rapids, Michigan as the city transforms itself into a scientific community and a medical mecca that seeks to attract the best minds from around the world.

Grand Rapids' Medical Mile is a cluster of prosperity. It stretches from the Grand Valley State University Cook-DeVos Center for Health Sciences that includes an entrepreneurial incubator on the east to Meijer Heart Center, Lemmen-Holton Cancer Pavilion, Spectrum-Butterworth Hospital, Van Andel Research Institute and Michigan State University College of Human Medicine on the west.

It is the epicenter of this 21st century revolution in the way this community is thought of, and more importantly in the way this community thinks of itself. Yet, it is only part of Grand Rapids' story of transformation.

None of this existed 15 years ago. It all began with a $1 billion endowment from Jay Van Andel, a man who was destined to suffer from Parkinson's, one of the diseases being investigated at the research institute that bears his name.

The philanthropic spirit of the Van Andel family and this kind of revolutionary transformation are really nothing new for Grand Rapids. The city's history is one of flux. Grand Rapidians have a wonderful sense of self-reliance and self-preservation.

We begin our story as Europeans begin to settle in West Michigan, pushing out the Native Americans who had called the region home, inventing a new community with a new agrarian culture.

Industry came to Grand Rapids on the strength of the Grand River after the land was sown with seed and farmers began growing crops. The agrarian society became an industrial society in much the same way, as Medical Mile came to the city on the shoulders of Michigan Street NE not replacing the industrial society as much as transforming it by building on its strengths.

Throughout the reinvention of this American community, we will see how generations of Grand Rapidians, through a shared vision and a willingness to give back to the community, have survived two World Wars, the Great Depression and are coming out of the Great Recession.

We will also see how the Medical Mile is changing the people of Grand Rapids as they invite or at least grudgingly accept people of different colors, creeds, nationalities and religions or perhaps no religion at all to become their neighbors. This too is the history of Grand Rapids. It has always been a much more diverse community than commonly acknowledged.

Last Chance Mile: The Reinvention of an American Community is really the story of the people of this community. We will join the leaders of Grand Rapids as they confront the collapse of their city's manufacturing base and work together to create this new life-science cluster of prosperity.

We will go inside Van Andel Institute, the Michigan State University College of Human Medicine, the West Michigan Science and Technology Initiative, Spectrum-Butterworth Hospital, Helen DeVos Children's Hospital, and the Meijer Heart Center on the Mile, meeting the people who are saving lives, people whose lives have been saved, and the people who are, at street level, transforming their community.

We will meet a medical school student who grew up shoveling gravel at his family's concrete company, along with an intern who discovered there was no better place for her family than West Michigan.

We will also meet a scientist who is building a new business on four feet of laboratory bench space, the researchers who are working on cures for cancer and neurological diseases, and a Grand Rapids high school student who dreams of becoming both a doctor and the first person in her family with a high school diploma.

We will also go to the cities of Wyoming and Kalamazoo to see that the Medical Mile is more than a $1.5 billion campus on the shoulders of Michigan Street NE, a mile of concrete in Grand Rapids, and we will learn that not everyone bought into the idea that they had to be on the Mile to be part of this new community.

We will see that the Medical Mile needs to be much more than that if it is to prosper, and we will also look to the future to see that Grand Rapids needs much more than the Medical Mile to become the community it needs to be in the 21st century.

PREFACE

THIS IS NOT THE book that I was planning to write. My focus was originally on the "Mom and Pop" businesses of Grand Rapids, but a conversation with The Right Place Inc. President Birgit Klohs changed my mind, shining a light on the real story of Grand Rapids, the story of Medical Mile.

I saw then that Medical Mile, this cluster of prosperity, the gem of Grand Rapids inside the community that has become a jewel of Michigan, was a 21st century reinvention story that was begging to be told.

Communities across Michigan and the Midwest are rebuilding and reinventing themselves following the Great Recession that was really a Depression in some cities. The story of the reinvention of this American community, Grand Rapids, Michigan and the people who are behind it contains multiple lessons that need to be learned across the U.S.

When I informed Birgit that a local TV station had reported that development had stalled on Medical Mile because the construction cranes had disappeared, she was outraged explaining to me the real action, the real excitement, the real development that the TV station had missed was going on inside the buildings on Medical Mile.

She told me of the crosspollination of research that was made possible by the collaboration of competitive institutions. We talked about how those institutions were reaching out around the world for scientists, technicians, researchers, health care professionals and students and why that wouldn't be possible without the Medical Mile itself.

That is when I knew this story had to be told. And that is what I have attempted to do, to take you inside the buildings on the section of Michigan Street NE between College and Division avenues that has become this $1.5 billion campus we call "Medical Mile" in Grand Rapids. I will also attempt to introduce you to this city that has become my adopted hometown, along with the people who have become my neighbors.

While I was researching this book it also became apparent to me for the first time that this was not the Grand Rapids I had moved into in 1990.

The reinvention of this American community is about more than Medical Mile. It is a work in progress. That is also part of the story that will be told in these pages.

Nothing matters more than the people who are reinventing Grand Rapids, Michigan both inside the buildings on Medical Mile and outside those institutions. They are in some cases billionaires, in other instances millionaires. They are also the scientists, entrepreneurs, and students who are the dreamers.

We can't forget about the hundreds of thousands of people who call West Michigan their home. Not only have they bought into the idea of a reinvented community, they are pushing it forward every day.

The common bond they all have is a shared vision. This is not only the story of the construction of buildings and infrastructure. This is the story of how the people inside and outside Medical Mile have been able to convert individual insight into collective insight, to borrow a phrase from *Reinventing Discovery, The New Era of Networked Science*, by Michael Nielsen.

This is also the story of lessons learned in the development of a cluster of prosperity and the knowledge that we have to be working on the next cluster while keeping in mind that Medical Mile is not going to reach its potential if we confine our thinking to Grand Rapids.

Medical Mile must become a concentric circle around the globe.

Let me begin by introducing you to Michigan Street NE.

CHAPTER ONE:
Building the Vision

MICHIGAN STREET NE DOESN'T sleep anymore. The people and the traffic of Medical Mile keep it awake from College to Division avenues. A full mile that slumbers but never snores. It is the insomniac of Grand Rapids.

Ambulances scream up and down Michigan Street's spine at all hours, while Aero Med helicopters fly over its head, bringing patients, doctors and organs for transplant to Spectrum-Butterworth Hospital.

The flow of people running across Michigan Street's shoulders never stops. Doctors, nurses, and technicians of all races, colors, and creeds all in scrubs, some flowered, some plain, some blue, arriving for work, leaving for home every eight, ten or 12 hours. They never stop crossing from the new multi-story parking garages that were built on the northern shoulders of the Mile to the huge, blue Helen DeVos Children's Hospital building that was added on to the colossus of Grand Rapids health care, Spectrum-Butterworth hospital.

Parents are inside DeVos Children's and Spectrum-Butterworth hospitals at all hours of the day and night praying that their children's hearts will continue beating just as this heart of the Medical Mile keeps ticking away, a silent metronome that keeps Michigan Street NE from closing its eyes.

Doctors and nurses race across the spine of the Mile before the lights change. Some of them run into Meijer Heart Center. This is where old hearts are exchanged for new, where lives begin again, where families grieve, where families celebrate. It is the building of second chances. It is yet another reason that Michigan Street NE can't sleep anymore. The Mile won't let it even doze.

When another day does dawn, Michigan Street can't even lay down beside the exhausted third-shift that will soon be home, or sit beside the thirsty third-shift toasting the end of a long night in bars promising them the happiest hours of the day from 7 a.m. to 11 a.m., or at least the best prices.

Michigan Street NE has no time to rest. The first shift is arriving for work, parking on the northern shoulders of this concrete animal, walking down its spine to work on the southern shoulders of this Mile that brought new life and new dreams to Grand Rapids, the second-largest Michigan community, a community that no longer feels intimidated by Detroit.

Michigan Street is speeding up as the sun rises in the east, so bright that drivers are forced to slow to a crawl as they drive into the burning orb that is too low for their visors and too bright to see the car ahead. Traffic nearly stops in the eastbound lanes of I-196, the Gerald R. Ford Freeway, named for the city's favorite son, Michigan's only entry into the Oval Office in Washington D.C.

This is the artery that pumps life from the east into the heart of the Medical Mile and gives electricity to the nerve endings that make Michigan Street NE live as no other concrete animal in Grand Rapids. It not only brings scrubs-wearing healthcare professionals, it carries Grand Valley State University students on RAPID buses from their Allendale campus to West Michigan's mecca of medical education. The founders of Medical Mile set the Michigan State University College of Human Medicine and the GVSU school of Allied Health Professions on Michigan Street's powerful northern shoulders. They don't compete. They cooperate. Yet, there is never any rest for Michigan Street NE.

From the west come more doctors, nurses, technicians, the custodians, the administrators who live in the suburbs along with more students. Some of the professionals drive to the Mile in their BMWs, some on motorcycles, some on scooters, some on bicycles, some just walking. They will all be on their feet for the rest of the day, caring, learning, keeping Michigan Street NE awake.

Entrepreneurs come from the west and the east on I-196, from the north and south on U.S. 131, some driving more than an hour to get to their four feet of bench space on the fifth floor of the Cook-DeVos Center for Health Sciences where they will build their dreams of a new business.

Van Andel Research Institute is on the southern shoulders of Michigan Street NE. This was the first building to come to life as the Mile was built. Researchers and scientists from around the world are inside this high-security building searching for the cures for cancer, Parkinson's and Alzheimer's, the diseases that plague mankind.

There is no sleep for Michigan Street NE.

It isn't just the pounding of the feet, the roar of the motorcycles, the whine of the scooters, the whispers of the hybrid vehicles, the air brakes of the buses, and the horns of the cars that keep Michigan Street NE from napping. It is the voices. Men, women, high school and college students, from all over the globe, who are speaking more than two-dozen different languages as they repair human bodies, comfort the grieving, celebrate the living and create new lives for themselves.

Michigan Street never sleeps because the Medical Mile never grows tired.

It is not easy being the patriarchal rock on which the family of Grand Rapids is building its future. There is the snow and ice of a West Michigan winter, the heat of a summer, the drenching rains of spring and fall. Rock salt is dumped on it in the winter as sharp blades tear at its back. Giant cracks and holes open up on its spine as the snow and ice melt; hot tar is poured into the potholes to keep this concrete artery open for another season. Michigan Street NE shrugs it all off.

It wasn't always like this. For decades, Michigan Street NE lived a sleepier, gentler, and but never a kinder life. That was before the Medical Mile woke it up. Grand Rapids is hoping Michigan Street NE never closes its eyes again.

Manufacturing in West Michigan was robust as the 20th century came to a close. The Grand Rapids region, which for federal purposes includes Muskegon and Holland, was outperforming the national economy in job creation.

We were not worried about our factories as the 20th century came to a close. Total employment grew 13-to-17 percent from 1980-to-2000.

Manufacturing, led by the office furniture and auto industries, soared with employment in that sector growing 12.3 percent from 1980 to 1985, more than 11 percent from 1985 to 1990, and 16.2 percent from 1990 to 1995.

Times were good. What could go wrong? We were about to find out.

Even though jobs were not a concern for most of us during those years, Grand Rapids City Hall was worried about its downtown district. John Logie, one of the longest serving mayors in the city's history, remarked at a city commission meeting that people coming out of the Amway Grand Plaza Hotel were asking where they could find the downtown district, obviously unaware they were standing in the middle of it.

One of downtown Grand Rapids' retail landmarks, Herpolsheimer's, the store you saw in the Tom Hanks animated movie "The Polar Express," was on its last legs. The store where President Gerald Ford met his wife Betty while she worked as a fashion coordinator, was about to close.

It was destined to become part of the failed attempt to reinvent downtown Grand Rapids. A developer bought the Herp's building, demolished the Gantos building—another downtown retail landmark-- and built an urban shopping mall, "City Center." It was downtown's answer to the suburban malls and their free parking—unfortunately without the free parking.

City Center opened in the mid-1980s complete with Herp's overhead train that was also part of "The Polar Express." The movie did a lot better than City Center. This experiment in downtown revitalization never took off. It didn't have the free parking, the stores, or the customers that the suburban malls had, and closed its doors six years later.

It was not as bad for Grand Rapids as the collapse of the auto industry theme park "Auto World" was for Flint. But, it was not good.

Most of the stores that were on the Monroe Mall in downtown Grand Rapids had moved to City Center, and when it closed, they left for the suburbs.

The Grand Rapids Police Department took over City Center, moving its headquarters into the facility. When you walk by now, you get the feeling this was either never intended to be a law enforcement building or it might have been designed by a police chief who loved Miami Vice.

In 1992, just as the office furniture and auto industry players in metro Grand Rapids were seeing some of their best years, downtown Grand Rapids was seeing some of its worst.

Downtown Grand Rapids, at the time was not much more than Monroe Mall, which had become a vacant pedestrian shopping mall occupied mainly by homeless beggars sleeping in doorways under signs that read "closed" or "for lease." However, there were "mom and pop," family-owned businesses that had been there for generations. They were surviving, but many like patients on Medical Mile should have been in the ICU.

City leaders decided to redesign Monroe Mall, and re-open it as "Monroe Center," taking away the pedestrian mall design and opening it up to cars, trucks and parking meters.

The construction killed the few mom-and-pops that were left standing. Monroe Center was ripped up, problems were found in the infrastructure below, we had to climb over mountains of dirt, splash through mud, and tip-toe over sheets of plywood covering holes in the ground, to get through the heart of the city's downtown.

Manufacturing in Grand Rapids was a few years behind, but its fall would be just as painful.

We never saw it coming.

The region's manufacturing employment was still growing, albeit more slowly from 1995 to 2000, but then the bottom just fell out with employment dropping by 18.5 percent the next five years. It was a hard landing.

We were about to learn some very tough lessons. We could no longer depend on a single industry or economic sector; we were no longer better than everyone else. We needed help.

We also were about to learn that we could depend on people like Rich DeVos, Jay Van Andel, and the others with money, the real money, in Grand Rapids. They turned philanthropy into an economic development force to be reckoned with. Those who had money gave money. That was a Grand Rapids tradition. They donated strategically, with a shared vision.

It was more than their money they gave Grand Rapids. It was also this shared vision. DeVos and Van Andel were new money, first generation millionaires at the time, destined to become billionaires. The ancestors of the people who founded one of the giants in metro Grand Rapids, Steelcase Inc., joined them. The Hunting, Pew, Cook and Wege families were second- and third-generation money in Grand Rapids. The head of Old Kent Bank, Dick Gillette was another leader of the renaissance movement.

They mobilized city and community leaders. But would it be enough?

The Grand Vision Committee that they had formed ahead of this storm was renamed Grand Action. It was decided Grand Rapids needed a convention center, an entertainment and sports arena and even a baseball team.

They also formed an economic development organization, The Right Place Inc. Its mandate covered metro Grand Rapids, but that was soon expanded to all of West Michigan. Taking a regional view of West Michigan from Grand Rapids to Holland to Muskegon was not the norm. This was a fresh idea. The wisdom of thinking regionally is one of the lessons learned on the Medical Mile.

The Right Place Inc. was soon followed by a group of business and community leaders forming the West Michigan Strategic Alliance. They made no apology for the belief that West Michigan had to see itself as a region rather than a patchwork of communities, each with its own agenda. This was an expansion of a very fresh idea.

Jay and Betty Van Andel took the philanthropic tradition to a new level. They tossed us a $1 billion lifeline in 1996. This endowment combined with public sector support created Van Andel Institute, the founding anchor of Medical Mile.

It was the gift of all gifts.

What would Grand Rapids do with it? The city has a history of being very parochial, provincial, and even unwelcoming. Its location is part of the problem. Grand Rapids just isn't close to anything of any significance except Lake Michigan.

Even though Grand Rapids is the second-largest city in Michigan, it has been dwarfed by Detroit and especially Metro Detroit. As a result, this West Michigan community has been on the short-end of the funding stick from Lansing and Washington. The region was also on the lower rungs of influence in the Michigan Legislature if only because it had so few state Representatives and Senators compared to Detroit.

West Michigan set itself up as being apart from Detroit. It has always been much more conservative religiously and politically. The region's business leaders always been proudly anti-union, offering that as an incentive for their colleagues outside of Grand Rapids to move to the region.

Those who were born and raised here, stayed here. Those who moved here often did not stay. I heard Steelcase CEO Jim Hackett tell a business audience close to the turn of the 21st century that while he had little trouble attracting young college graduates to Grand Rapids, he was hard pressed to keep them here longer than a year, especially if they weren't white.

The standing joke in Grand Rapids is, "if you aren't Dutch, you aren't much." That was meant as a joke but it is the kind of attitude that some warned could cripple this billion dollar gift that this American community had been given. Yet it still produced a laugh along with a knowing shoulder shrug.

With a shock that threatened the foundation of the community, that paradigm changed in the 1990s. Our children started leaving and staying away. Would we be able to reverse that? Would we be able to offer them a real future? Would their lives be better than ours? That is the dream of all parents. We were also starting to worry about our own futures.

There were also some worrisome questions being asked by those who shared a new vision for this American community. Would we be able to realize the potential of Medical Mile on our own? Would we be able to really open our arms and our communities to the rest of the world? How about growing another generation to take Medical Mile to the next stage if we do manage to shepherd it to success this time? And how would we judge that success?

As Medical Mile was opening, we asked ourselves several questions about the creation of the reinvention of this American community.

What did we want out of Medical Mile? Did we really want to become a magnet for medical care and life sciences, bringing with it people who don't act the way we do, dress the way we do, eat the same foods, speak the same language or even worship the same God?

Should we be careful what we wished for?

These were all open questions when the first ground was broken and Van Andel Institute was built on Michigan Street. They were questions we really could not take time to answer because our local economy was in such a state of collapse.

The Old Order was falling in on itself. It had happened in Detroit, a city with a flamboyant mayor, Kwame Kilpatrick, who was destined to land in a prison cell. The city of more than a million powered by the auto industry was soon to have less than 800-thousand people calling it home, with enough vacant land to house the city of San Francisco. Detroit Mayor Dave Bing would begin turning off street lights and city services in neighborhoods deemed hopeless in an effort to herd the remaining population into salvageable streets. We were scared to death it could happen to us.

And finally, would the lessons we learn on the Mile be transferable to other areas, to the next stage of Grand Rapids' and West Michigan's development, or is this as good as it gets?

Grand Rapids was built on the banks of the Grand River by the furniture industry that came to West Michigan on the power of the Grand River. Grand Rapids was hoping, as the 21st century dawned, that Medical Mile that was being built on the shoulders of Michigan Street would create a new, more sustainable community.

Grand Rapids was facing an awakening to a new economic reality. But truth be told, Grand Rapids had been through this before. The largest city in West Michigan, the second largest municipality in Michigan, had seen what the urban studies theorist Richard Florida describes as the Long Depression of the 1870s, to be followed by the Great Depression of the 1930s and the Great Recession of the 21st century.

Grand Rapids had even had city hall scandals, like the Great Water Scandal in the early 1900s. It involved a scheme to profit from bonds sold to finance a project to bring Lake Michigan water to Grand Rapids. Before it was wrapped up, it would reach from New York, to Chicago, to Omaha and of course to Grand Rapids. A mayor, fourteen aldermen, the city attorney, the city clerk, a state senator, an ex-prosecutor, leaders in society, church and business, the publishers of three newspapers, and even some court officials were caught up in this storm.

Grand Rapids had created industries that manufactured everything from furniture to flypaper, from beer to auto parts. Most had disappeared. Office furniture manufacturers and auto industry suppliers were barely hanging on. What hope did Medical Mile and its life sciences promise for the future really hold for Grand Rapids? Would this be another City Center-like failure, or would it be a real cluster of prosperity?

Would Grand Rapids be able to change itself enough to morph from a predominately white, very conservative community of blue collars and colleges to an even more diverse, accepting community?

Grand Rapidians have always had a real instinct for self-preservation. They are not strangers to reinvention. But this time they created something truly special. Medical Mile would become Michigan's largest life sciences cluster, responsible for 46,000 direct and indirect jobs and $4.4 billion gross regional product.

It is as exceptional as the invention of the community that would become Grand Rapids, Michigan.

CHAPTER TWO:
Invention of an American Community

THERE WAS NEVER A day when Sophie de Marsac Campau did not wake up to hardship and loneliness.

Her childhood probably ended as it did for most girls in the 1800s, at the age of 14. After that it was day after day of toil. Water was boiled and clothes were washed, by hand, in that hot, hot water. If she was lucky, she had a hand-operated washing machine. Like most women, she probably just had a washboard.

Dirt was everywhere. Dust was on everything. Dust from the dirty paths that passed for streets, dust from the dried manure that fell from horses. Flies and the diseases they carried were everywhere. Thick clouds of flies were attracted by outhouses, latrine trenches and mounds of garbage behind Grand Rapids homes.

Louis Campau, met and married Sophie in Detroit, then brought her to what would become Grand Rapids, Michigan in 1827. He put food on their table by establishing a trading post.

Sophie spoke only French. The Indian women spoke their own language. The "Yankee" women who came before her spoke only English.

Sophie only had one friend. Mrs. Slater, the missionary's wife, who spoke no French, but able to communicate with Sophie through a kind of sign language they created. They never spoke a word. What good would that have done?

Another day spent in Grand Rapids.

Aside from her husband, those sign-language conversations were the only human interaction Sophie had in this God-forsaken wilderness that Louis had decided to make their home.

This lesson Sophie learned would be handed down through generations of Grand Rapidians: if you are going to make it, you are going to make it on your own. The people of West Michigan are for the most part a very self-reliant breed. It is in their DNA. If you are first-generation, you pick it up through osmosis. Thought and culture molecules are everywhere. Grand Rapids doesn't keep its norms and mores secret.

Another lesson learned that would prove to be very transferable to those who followed the Campau family was the lesson of capitalism, though it wasn't known by that name in Sophie and her husband's day. They were just making a living.

Louis, who would become one of the founders of Grand Rapids, was a fur trader. That only went so far. Campau made money however he could. Louis was a businessman above all else who woke up every day knowing that it was up to him to provide for himself and his incredibly lonely wife, Sophie.

Louis was just as much an outsider as Sophie, as were the Yankee men and women who preceded them. But he carved out a place for himself in what would become Grand Rapids. His log huts and trading post were the first scars on the wilderness that before him and his people was unspoiled.

He was also more than just a fur trading, whiskey-selling business man. He was what generations after him would call, an entrepreneur. The people who built Medical Mile were no less a pioneer than Louis, and he was no less an entrepreneur.

Two other men who would become legends in Grand Rapids also brought their families, along with their dreams and ambitions. Louis, Lucius Lyon and John Ball were to form an uneasy alliance -- a triad of founding, development and promotion that would create the town that would be known as Grand Rapids.

Life never got any easier for Sophie. Her husband's power and influence couldn't buy her a friend. West Michigan's weather didn't make her life any easier. There are more cloudy days than sunny days in Grand Rapids, far more.

Their winters-- and ours today-- can be brutal. The summers are broiling and humid. The spring and autumn offer only a few months of relief.

Sophie, Louis and the rest of the people of Grand Rapids had to deal with the torrential rains of spring and summer, along with the melting winter snow that forced them to wade ankle-deep through the mud, slop and horse manure to shop, to live, merely to exist.

It wasn't like the native women of Grand Rapids had it any easier. Louis, Sophie and even Rev. and Mrs. Slater brought them nothing but misery in a bottle. They brought them alcohol.

Blame this on people like Louis, a man memorialized as one of the great founders of Grand Rapids, a man who also can shoulder much of the blame for what became of the native people who had lived their lives, raised their families, created their community before Louis and Sophie had ever dreamed of Grand Rapids

Louis sold them liquor. Nothing stopped him or the other traders. He was said to be able to sell ten barrels of whiskey in one night.

Native Grand Rapids men lost their pride and their dignity because of the liquor that Louis and those like him sold them. The women lost more. They lost their noses.

Some historians blame that on women, drunk on whiskey, fighting each other, until one had a nose bitten completely off. Other say cutting off the nose of a women caught cheating on her husband was tribal punishment. There was also the influence of whiskey. No matter the cause, there were a lot of women without noses.

Louis, who knew the native people of Grand Rapids before he corrupted them, is credited with telling the story of their collective fate:

"A few white men came and there was little trouble. A few more white men arrived and there was more trouble. Then a lot came and the Indians became bad. Finally the Indians were relieved of their possessions."[1]

Life was never easy. Mrs. William Almy Richmond and her family had to run from their dinner table one evening to escape the water that overflowed the banks of the Grand River and flooded their home.

"Under the boot and the hoof and the groaning wheel there came to be quagmire that had no chance to restore itself, and the beauty of the scene faded more," she wrote to relatives. "After a while the mud flowed down Monroe like lava."

The Grand River was friend and foe alike for those who founded and settled in Grand Rapids. The city got its name from the Indian word for the waterway, Owashtanong[2], that brought the Indians fish, and whose power

---

1   Z.Z. Lydens, editor, *The Story of Grand Rapids*, (Grand Rapids: Kregel Publications, 1966), 2

2   Z.Z. Lydens, editor, *The Story of Grand Rapids*, (Grand Rapids: Kregel Publications, 1966), 2

brought the logs that created the furniture industry and the village that sprung up around those factories.

The river was powerful, flooding much of what was to become downtown Grand Rapids in 1838. The streets were jammed with ice cakes and the town was almost completely submerged. Because of a flood in 1852, boats were able to float on what is now Market Street.

A 1904 flood caused more than $1 million in property damage. But, the Great Log Jam of 1883 is the best example of the power of the Grand River and the furniture industry coming to loggerheads.

More than 150-million feet of logs were jammed in the Grand River. Nothing moved until heavy rains inundated the city, the Grand River rose, the jam was broken, and the logs roared down the Grand River breaking up every bridge in their path.

You have to wonder why Lucius, Louis, and John were so committed to this site. Grand Rapids was not the only town along the Grand River. The settlement that would become Grandville was just downriver, and it had the advantage of being level. The ground around the bend in the river that would become the city of Grand Rapids was incredibly hilly, almost mountainous for West Michigan.

Yet, there is one thing about the Grand Rapidians of that day. When they put their minds to something they did it. They cut through the hills to build the streets that would form downtown Grand Rapids and would give rise to the seven neighborhoods of what is now known as the Michigan Street Corridor, "visited by 1.25 million people annually" according to Grand Rapids city planners.

Lucius Lyon and Louis Campau competed mightily for control of what would become Grand Rapids. Campau purchased a large piece of land in 1831 that, if you believe in destiny, was fated to be the heart of what would become downtown Grand Rapids. It is now bounded by Division Avenue, Fulton Street and Michigan Street, the latter of which would become the most important thoroughfare in Grand Rapids less than two centuries later.

But Lyon was not to be outdone by Campau. He immediately bought a section of land at the north side of Campau's land. So Campau platted his tract in a way that forced Lyon to dead-end the streets of his sections against the cross-streets of the Campau plat. That prevented Lyon from reaching the all- important Grand River with his streets.

What a mess. The Campau/Lyon struggle went so far as to impact the name of the city and the name of what would be the county of Kent. The village was called Grand Rapids at Campau's request. But Lyon used his political muscle to get the post office named Kent, the name he had put on his plat of land. The Indians called Lyon "the Fox."[3]

Somehow they invented this American community without killing each other. No duels were fought, at least not with pistols. Both men planted their flags and they really did change the land that would be known as Grand Rapids.

Campau, Lyon and the rest who are memorialized with street names and statues in Grand Rapids may have been among the first. They were far from the last.

More people of vision were destined to come down the Grand River, bringing industry and commerce to Grand Rapids, moving it away from its agrarian past, just as another generation would come from around the world and would move down Michigan Street to reinvent this American community once again.

---

3   Z.Z. Lydens, editor, *The Story of Grand Rapids*, (Grand Rapids: Kregel Publications, 1966) 9-16

Chapter Three:
The Furniture City is Born

WILLIAM WIDDICOMB MUST HAVE been a nice guy. He cared about his employees, the craftsmen (never women) in his factory on the northeast side of Grand Rapids, as he would members of an extended family.

Legend has it that all of the owners of the Grand Rapids furniture factories valued their employees that way. Widdicomb is said to have granted an employee a day off in 1900 to prepare for the christening of his newborn son.

Widdicomb even gave that man and hundreds of employees after him, christening gowns for the baby girls and boys born to the furniture titan's extended family.

Widdicomb was second-generation rich. His father, George, did not come to Grand Rapids as a rich man. The elder Widdicomb was an Englishman, a cabinet maker, a craftsman. So he understood the men who worked in his factory. He was one of them.

George Widdicomb was the kind of pure Americana success story that Grand Rapids has always loved. He worked as a cabinet maker at the Winchester Brothers' factory, spinning off his own shop that he ran with his four sons, George Junior, Harry, John and William.

George Sr. retired, George Jr. died, and the three surviving brothers started a factory on Fifth Street NW, Grand Rapids. John Widdicomb then spun off his own business, John Widdicomb Co., and built another factory, which became a bricks-and-mortar icon for Grand Rapids.

But it also became one of the facilities that Grand Rapids just didn't know what to do with in the latter years of the 20th century. It was another of the great, old factories that were empty except for the vermin and the homeless who had no place else to go.

A city like Grand Rapids would never let that continue. And it did not. The buildings that housed the John Widdicomb Co., Berkey and Gay, the Globe and more have all been reinvented as condominium spaces; office, residential and retail.

However that was more than 100 years in the future. In the 19th century, the Widdicomb family and hundreds of craftsmen were creating the furniture that would make Grand Rapids America's "Furniture City."

This idyllic story came to a crashing end on a spring evening in 1911 when decades of pent-up anger broke loose and sparked a riot as those craftsmen and their families turned their fury on the Widdicomb family and the other furniture industry barons.

Even though the average factory worker in the furniture industry of the 19th and early 20th centuries saw himself as far more than a mere assembler of furniture, the craftsmen's lives were not easy. Early to work and early to rise wasn't a lifestyle choice, it was a necessity. Factory whistles blew at ear-ripping decibels to make sure that the men who would spend ten-hours a day inside the plants got to work on time.

Of course with that kind of an incentive, no one in those neighborhoods overslept. The whole family was up at 5:30 a.m. The husband got ready for work. The wife made his breakfast, packed his lunch and off he went. Home for supper, and then off to a church or a lodge meeting that would start at 7:30 p.m. Back to bed and up again. That was the life of a factory worker in Grand Rapids.

It was not just the men who lived this life at the turn of the 20th century. It was also the boys. Just as with the girls of Sophie Campau's generation, the carefree life of a boy ended early. Twelve-year olds were often put to work in the factories and many stayed for the rest of their lives. What other choice did they have?

More than four-hundred men and boys would rise with the Widdicomb Fifth Street factory whistle and walk through their west side neighborhood to work in the building that would become such an important thread in Grand Rapids' industrial fabric.

There were problems. The workers were not happy. The furniture companies were bringing in indentured labor to take the jobs of Grand Rapids men. Conditions inside the furniture plants were very bad, sub-standard even for the late 19th century and early 20th century.

In April 1911, craftsmen turned on craftsmen, with their wives and children by their side. The Widdicomb family became collateral damage, and the Great Grand Rapids Furniture Strike was on.

Hundreds of Polish craftsmen, their wives and their children gathered at the Widdicomb factory on the northwest side of Grand Rapids, all strikers. They had done the unthinkable. They had walked off the job in one of the three great strikes that ripped the Grand Rapids furniture industry and the Grand Rapids community apart, as some vocal church leaders took sides in the disputes.

Tempers this night were at a boiling point. Strike-breakers had kept the Widdicomb factory open. When they left work, the strikers and their families were waiting for them, along with a hail of head-breaking, face-tearing stones.

The women and children formed a human shield to protect their striking husbands, sons and fathers when police arrived to break it up. The fire department came and turned their hoses on the strikers and their families. It was not enough. The strikers and their families didn't leave until they had broken every window in the factory. [4]

His father may have thought of them as his extended family, handing out christening gowns to new fathers, but in the months leading up to the strike, Harry Widdicomb had come out of his office one day, waving a gun at the labor organizers. The animosity ran both ways and on the night of the riot, Harry had to run for his life. His employees hated him.

The perception that Widdicomb workers were like members of the Widdicomb family was replaced with the reality of labor vs. management conflict.

No matter the root causes of the conflict, the fact remained that families like the Widdicombs had built the furniture industry in Grand Rapids. Why here? What was it about this place that made it the perfect spot for this industrial cluster?

It was the power of the Grand River, the unrelenting power of the river, which unrestrained led to devastating floods in what is now downtown Grand Rapids. It also had the force to bring untold numbers of logs to Grand Rapids. The dense woods and timber mills upriver sent lumber floating down to this bend in the river, where the factories along its banks could scoop their raw materials from the water, turn it into furniture, and then send it down the river to rail heads and the harbor of Grand Haven on Lake Michigan. From there, it could be shipped anywhere.

Yet, the furniture industry didn't stay on the banks of the Grand

---

4   Jeffrey D. Kleiman, *Strike! How the Furniture Workers Strike of 1911 Changed Grand Rapids*, (Grand Rapids: Grand Rapids Historical Commission, 2006), 93-95

River for long. As soon as the transportation infrastructure improved, as soon as the trains came, the industry moved as close to the railroad tracks as possible. That was a lesson to be learned and never forgotten. It also became critical in the evolution of Medical Mile. The lesson is simply this: infrastructure rules the day. Whoever has the best will win.

Grand Rapids' furniture first gained national prominence at the Philadelphia Centennial Exposition in 1876. Eastern buyers started making a pilgrimage to Grand Rapids and in less than twenty years as many as 100 purchasing agents were making the thousand- mile trip every year.

The furniture industry became a very active, very real cluster of prosperity in Grand Rapids just as the Medical Mile would a century later.

However, history also shows us that just because an industry cluster is created; it does not necessarily follow that it will become a cluster of prosperity. Take for instance piggeries, a short-lived effort to systematize what had been a natural way to dispose of garbage. Grand Rapidians would throw their uneaten food out the back door. Wild animals would eat it. It was nature's way. It worked until so many people moved into Grand Rapids that too much garbage was created for even the wild animals to eat. The piggery concept was born.

Feeding uneaten and spoiled food to pigs was not the first option. When the odor of piled up garbage and the vermin that feasted on it became too much to bear, it was thrown into the Grand River. So much was tossed into that waterway that in 1895 the Army Corps of Engineers said floating garbage had become a navigation hazard.[5]

Alvah Brown had the solution. He signed a $1,200 contract with the city of Grand Rapids to haul away its garbage. It is possible that Alvah neglected to tell city leaders what he was doing with it. Perhaps they didn't ask.

He was trucking it to what is now a southeast side Grand Rapids neighborhood, at Alger and Plymouth, where he cooked the garbage, mixed it with water, and fed it to 500 pigs. But the smell of that proved so atrocious that Brown was forced to move his operation into the countryside.

Two other agribusiness entrepreneurs soon formed their own piggery operations, and Grand Rapids had its first piggery cluster.

---

5   Linda Samuelson, Andrew Schrier, et a., Heart & Soul, *The Story of Grand Rapids Neighborhoods*, (William B. Eerdmans Publishing Co. 2003) 61

But Grand Rapids failed to become the Piggery City. The garbage the pigs were eating made their pork taste so bad, that the pigs could not be sold to pork producers. Enter the practice of the chemical incineration of garbage.

This was not the first, nor the last of the business clusters that have come and gone in Grand Rapids. The list includes wagon wheels, bicycles, beer, knitted products like underwear for U.S. troops, even gas-resistant underwear in 1943, flour mills, the manufacture of bricks, the mining of gypsum.

Beer was making a huge comeback as *Last Chance Mile* went to press. Grand Rapids and Asheville, North Carolina tied for the title of "Beer City USA" in a non-scientific poll.[6]

Furniture was the first cluster that gave Grand Rapids a worldwide identity and it still gives the community a sense of identity, although the health care community far surpasses it in terms of revenue, gross regional product and employment.

By the 1930s the Grand Rapids furniture industry was alive, well and bustling. At its zenith, there were 13,000 skilled workers making their livings in 68 furniture factories. Trains took chairs, tables, desks and beds to market around the nation. Boats took hutches and more down the Grand River to freighters waiting in Lake Michigan.

Grand Rapids would eventually lose its place as the home of furniture manufacturing but would hold on to its role for a time as the center of furniture design.

Because it was a true cluster of prosperity, the furniture industry brought not only the craftsmen who built the furniture; it brought the designers who would become world-renowned and the retailers who created a new way to sell furniture.

That is another lesson that this cluster of prosperity taught Grand Rapids, a lesson that would be reinforced on the Medical Mile. Talent attracts talent.

However, that was only one industry cluster that would take Grand Rapids by storm in the 1930s. More than 21,000 people, mostly men,

---

6   Garret Ellison, "Beer City USA Poll Results: Grand Rapids ties with Asheville. Now what?" *M-Live.com, The Grand Rapids Press,* May 14, 2012. Accessed May 14, 2012. http://www.mlive.com/business/west-michigan/index. ssf/2012/05/beer_city_usa_poll_results_gra.html

were working in 387 factories of all kinds, earning a total of $25 million a year.

It was the Grand Rapids furniture industry, though, that soared to such heights that the Seventh Circuit Court of Appeals in Chicago ruled in 1942 that a company in Chicago could not use the name, "Grand Rapids Furniture Co." because "…the words 'Grand Rapids furniture' have acquired in the trade a special significance, and furniture made in that city is held by a large part of the purchasing public to be superior in design, workmanship and value to furniture usually purchased elsewhere."

The owners, craftsmen and designers of the furniture industry brought more than commerce to Grand Rapids. They left a lasting legacy of conservative religious and political beliefs along with a strong work ethic that was admired by industrialists across the United States.

They also taught the city and the region transferable lessons in the way labor and industry would relate—for good and bad—along with the need for constant innovation, and the need for collaboration and partnerships.

The titans of the furniture industry had changed Grand Rapids. George Widdicomb, Elias Matters, James and Ezra Nelson, C.C. Comstock, Charles R. Sligh, George W. Gay, and the Berkey brothers, Julius and William all made their fortunes building furniture in Grand Rapids.

But they really built more. They invented and reinvented this American community's culture. That is what lasted.

Their factories would close in the 20th century and sit vacant for decades. But the buildings were constructed to last. They still exist and are still useful, finding reinvention, renovation and reuse as residential and office space, thanks to the vision of state and city leaders, along with the Grand Rapids business community.

We also learned the lesson that sometimes perception does not equal reality. As big as the furniture industry seemed to Grand Rapids, it was really never huge.

"It really had been a cottage industry for a century," said industry analyst Michael Dunlap. Its history is more a study of craftsmanship than mass production.

In the end, Grand Rapids, once known by the world as "Furniture City," with enough company names to fill several pages in this book, was left with only office furniture. Steelcase, Herman Miller and Haworth are the Big Three of that industry, small businesses compared to the Detroit Three automakers.

We also learned the lesson from the legacy of the furniture industry that nothing lasts forever and we must always be preparing a new generation of business and community leaders.

The furniture industry in Grand Rapids was destined to be dwarfed by the health care industry and the Medical Mile. But first two Grand Rapids area men came on to the scene, high school buddies, boyhood friends who together created a global, mass-marketing phenomenon selling soap.

Rich DeVos and Jay Van Andel did more than sell soap. They sold a vision. Their children would try to use that vision to change the way Grand Rapids saw itself, and the way the world saw Grand Rapids. They would reinvent this American community.

CHAPTER FOUR:
Amway: The Foundation

GRAND RAPIDS' ECONOMY WAS starting to seize up in the 1990s. It had happened before, but never like this. The last decade of the 20th century brought a real culture shock that rocked out lives.

The 1970s were tough on Michigan. The Arab oil embargo hit us hard. However, we still believed that our high school diplomas were our tickets to a lifestyle at least as good as our parents' and we still believed that things were going to get better.

When the calendar turned 2000 it was different. This was a collapse. This was not cyclical. This was systemic. What we had been doing since the city was founded –blue-collar, lunch-bucket manufacturing--had gone all wrong. It just wasn't working anymore.

Grand Rapids manufacturing–furniture and auto -- was suddenly locked in a global battle for survival. People who kept their jobs never knew how long the paychecks would last. Those who lost a job couldn't be sure when or if they would be working again. But still we held on to the idea that things would get better. That was one of the lasting, transferable lessons that had been taught by the generations who came before us. However, it was a lesson that would have to be reinvented with the creation of Medical Mile.

The lesson taught to us by our parents, and to them by their parents, that things are going to get better, never died in Grand Rapids. No matter how bad it got, hope never faded that things would get better. To understand that, to understand West Michigan, you have to understand Amway Corp.

And to understand Amway, you have to understand Rich DeVos and Jay Van Andel, two conservative, religious men who mirrored the beliefs of their community.

They were best friends at Grand Rapids Christian High School, separated only by World War Two. Rich and Jay stayed in touch through those years and almost as soon as they arrived home, they opened a flight school that mostly catered to military veterans who wanted to learn how to fly.

Military veterans also get hungry. Sensing an ancillary business opportunity, the Van Andel-DeVos team also opened a drive-in restaurant to feed their students, serving butter-fried hamburgers, using their mothers' recipe.

Jay and Rich were also taught a lesson that almost all entrepreneurs on the Medical Mile may have to learn. Failure is a part of the experience. Neither of their first businesses did very well. Both were sold. Jay and Rich didn't stop. They began another adventure.

Even though Jay and Rich were the first to admit they knew nothing about sailing, the pair set off for South America in 1949 on the schooner, "Elizabeth." It sank off the shore of Cuba. The pair had to be rescued by an American freighter. They eventually made their way to South America.

Was this yet another DeVos-Van Andel failure? The answer was "no," at least not as far as they were concerned.

"That is part of our folklore," Steve Van Andel, one of Jay's four children, told me. "For most people, once the boat sank, it would be the end of the story. For them it was just half-way through (the journey)."

The logic is astoundingly simple. "Their boat had taken them as far as they needed it to take them. They didn't need that boat anymore."

Steve still has the bell from the "Elizabeth" in his office at Amway Corp. where he serves as chairman of the corporation his father and Rich created, sharing leadership duties with one of Rich DeVos' sons, Doug, who is Amway's president.

"People may say 'Rich and Jay were great visionaries' but they were just trying to feed their families. And our dads would even say, 'all we did was go to work every day,'" Doug explained as he, Steve and I spent an hour together in Amway's Ada Township corporate offices. "But they went to work every day with an attitude that they were going to make the business better."

Amway had a humble birth in 1959, launched in the basement of Jay's home, selling a product billed as "an all-purpose household cleaner." Hardly glamorous, but this was the business that would make them billionaires.

"It was 1959, when it was Castro versus the United States and communism versus free enterprise," said Doug. "Freedom was an idea they wanted to have a piece of."

A direct selling and manufacturing operation, Amway (which is meant to be an abbreviation for "American Way") eventually went global with annual sales of $9.2 billion at the end of 2010.

Jay was an enthusiastic donor to the Republican Party, giving $2 million to Progress for America, an organization that in the last three weeks leading up to the November 2004 outspent the next largest spending Democratic 527 group three-to-one on political ads. It bought $16.8 million worth of television and radio ad time.

He also, as did Rich, donated generously to Grand Rapids charities and cultural institutions, along with funding an Arizona facility that hoped to use scientific methods to prove the world was created by a supreme being in six days.

Just like his best friend, Rich DeVos spent his life in Grand Rapids. In addition to co-founding Amway, Rich also owns the NBA Orlando Magic franchise. And like Van Andel, Rich has been generous to a fault in his donations to a variety of charities and cultural institutions in Grand Rapids.

Rich also became very active in Republican Party politics. I heard him tell a business group in Grand Rapids that he started donating money to the GOP as soon as he learned that was how the game was played.

DeVos and Van Andel also created a new spirit of philanthropy when they led the fundraising effort to rehabilitate the old Pantlind Hotel in downtown Grand Rapids, an iconic landmark, the focal point, of downtown Grand Rapids for generations.

The Pantlind survived the hob-nailed boots of the men who guided the logs down the Grand Rapids, the lumber needed by the furniture industry and carpenters making their livings in the city. The nails on their boots that allowed them to dance from log to log were so sharp and strong they tore the planks of the boardwalk along the River into match sticks. But a resourceful employee at the Pantlind invented warm, furry, sock-like slippers and convinced the log drivers to exchange their boots for more comfortable footwear.

This is another lesson learned that has been transferred from generation to generation in Grand Rapids: Necessity is the mother of many inventions and you can always make it better.

However, as majestic as it was, the Pantlind could not fight the impact of time. It needed to be rehabilitated. DeVos led the fundraising drive, but found he could not raise a penny until he formed a public-private partnership with the city of Grand Rapids. He had to have some skin in the game, too.

DeVos eventually succeeded. His company's name went up on the side of the Amway Grand Plaza Hotel.

No one who spent any time in Grand Rapids during the last two decades of the 20th century could have any doubts about Rich's religious or political beliefs. He was an outspoken opponent of gay marriage and same-sex health care benefits, especially on the campus of Grand Valley State University.

He told *The Grand Rapids Press* in 1990, "…I deal with a lot of wonderful gay people. I hire a lot of them. …I respect them. I am good friends with them. But you live your life the way you want to live and I'll live mine…But don't keep trying to change things. That's all."

That is what Richard Florida wrote about in The Rise of the Creative Class. It pretty much was as good as it got when I moved into Grand Rapids. That is why Advocate.com ranking Grand Rapids in January 2012 as one of the Gayest Cities in America came as such a surprise and why I see it as evidence of the reinvention of this American community. This is not the Grand Rapids I moved into in 1990.

Grand Rapids could not be what it is today without the second generations of the DeVos and Van Andel families staying in the city and staying true to the mission of their fathers. This was not accidental. This was done with real purpose.

In the mid-1990s when power was being transferred to the second generation, Doug and Steve asked their fathers to sit down and put their fundamentals and ideals in writing.

That conversation led to the words that Amway lives by; the Founders' Fundamentals: Freedom, Family, Hope and Reward and the Amway corporate values: Partnership, Integrity, and Personal Worth, Personal Responsibility, Freedom and Free Enterprise.

Those founding principles and corporate values are Amway. They are also Grand Rapids.

"The 'foundations' are really more than just foundations for the business," Steve explained. "They are really the foundations that both of them (Jay and Rich) built their lives around. They are the foundations they taught us and they are the foundations that are the fabric of our families and who we are."

The furniture industry created millionaires. Amway made Rich DeVos and Jay Van Andel billionaires. They were ranked consistently among the world's richest people but they never forgot Grand Rapids.

Neither have the second- and third-generations of their families.

David Van Andel is running Van Andel Institute, and is helping to guide the evolution of Medical Mile. Steve Van Andel and Doug DeVos are at the helm of Amway and are woven into the Grand Rapids community. Rich DeVos' other son, Dick, is also highly involved in Grand Rapids and ran for Governor against Jennifer Granholm.

Dick's son, Rich's grandson, Rick has had an incredible impact on Grand Rapids, creating "ArtPrize" a non-juried competition that brings artists from around the world to the city and hundreds of thousands of tourists.

Rick is more than ArtPrize. He is at the forefront of the new generation of Grand Rapids entrepreneurs leading their city into business, cultural and social arenas where it could not have dreamed of going in 1990.

The DeVos and Van Andel families are having an incredible impact on the reinvention of this American community.

Doug believes Medical Mile is a manifestation of "this culture of innovation (in West Michigan)."

This is why the idea that "it is going to get better," is so important to the creation of the Medical Mile: when you think the future is going to get better, you are willing to invest in the future.

One can't happen without the other. "That is part of the issue we have today in this country," said Steve. "There are so many people who do not have an optimistic view of the future, that all of a sudden things seize up a little bit."

Steve believes you tend to hit what you are aiming at. "And if you are aiming low that is probably where you are going to go. But if you aim high, you are probably going to go there. I think as a business you need to keep aiming up and you will eventually get there.'"

Doug agreed the belief that things will get better, and if you aim high you will score high, are the basic, core entrepreneurial beliefs that are driving Medical Mile.

"But you could apply it to any business or any industry. There are a lot of people doing it right now, people who are building a better mousetrap, coming up with a better idea," he said. "Look at our iPads and with Steve Jobs passing, we celebrate the way that entrepreneurial spirit thought of a way we could live our lives better.

There are a lot of people doing that right now, we just have not heard about them yet."

The belief that 'things are going to get better' has a lot to do with what is happening on Medical Mile, according to Steve.

"Think about where it has come from. It was not all that long ago when we had a hospital down there, and that was it. There was not a whole lot else," he said. "But as a community we decided that although we have some great businesses, we were having some tough times and we needed to invest in the future. I think to a large degree that is where the concept of the Mile came from."

One phone call, from Steve's brother Dave, to The Right Place Inc. President Birgit Klohs let the rest of Grand Rapids in on the secret. This American community was about to be reinvented.

CHAPTER FIVE:
Creating the Cluster

The Medical Mile's development was launched with a phone call from Dave Van Andel to The Right Place Inc. President Birgit Klohs. It was a phone call that would open the door to the Medical Mile, and open Grand Rapids' eyes to possibilities that most of us had not even dreamed of.

It was hardly a spur-of-the-moment decision. A shared vision never is. It doesn't just happen. It takes work. It takes planning. The leaders of the business and health care communities had been working on this concept for at least 20 years before the words "Medical Mile" became part of the Grand Rapids vocabulary.

One of the lessons Medical Mile teaches us is that a shared vision, if it is going to be sustainable, requires research, planning and development. The early-stage players in the creation of Medical Mile did all of that. They also understood that to be sustainable, the Mile had to have much more than what was on Michigan Street NE when the discussions began. This new cluster of prosperity had to include a medical school, a research institute, and a platform to grow entrepreneurs who would be launching life sciences and medical device businesses.

Michigan Street NE and all of Grand Rapids also had to be willing to embrace a new attitude. The 21st century was knocking at our door. It was time to let it in.

Hospitals we had. A medical school we needed. A research institute was essential. The electricity that gave Medical Mile a jumpstart was the decision by Jay and Betty Van Andel to set up a $1 billion endowment to create one of those pieces, Van Andel Institute. Their son, Dave Van Andel, placed a phone call to economic developer Birgit Klohs, the president of The Right Place Inc. and told her that it was going to happen.

That phone call opened the door for the reinvention of this American community.

"I am looking at this from an economic development standpoint now. We are marketing this community as a life sciences attractor, as a life sciences cluster. Fifteen or 16 short years ago that would have been a non-starter," she said as we sat in the conference room of The Right Place Inc. (RPI) offices in the Waters Building, another of the historic structures in downtown Grand Rapids.

I have known Birgit for those 15 or 16 years and have always seen her as Grand Rapids' link to the rest of the world. Her home language is German. She has lectured in her homeland, along with France, Great Britain, China, Sweden, Australia, Israel and of course the U.S.

Birgit had a tight relationship with Michigan's first women governor, Jennifer Granholm, joining her on many overseas trade missions. They were two of our economic development warriors who not only worked at attracting new businesses from around the world to Grand Rapids and Michigan, but also did their best to push and prod us forward to join the global community.

Times were not good in Michigan. Manufacturing was dying. The auto plants were closing in Detroit. The white and middle-class flight from the Motor City was slowing only because there were so few people left. Furniture factories were shutting down in West Michigan. Middle managers who had been moving the industries of Grand Rapids forward were now helping children cross the street to school.

Manufacturing would no longer be the top employer in Grand Rapids. Spectrum Health Systems was number-one, followed by Meijer Inc., the retail giant of West Michigan. The media was filled with stories of the death of manufacturing, the death of a high-school diploma as a ticket to a middle-class lifestyle, and the death of life as we knew it in Grand Rapids and in Michigan.

Michigan (just like the street that bears its name in Grand Rapids) was built on the blue-collared shoulders of manufacturing, the heavy metal giant that had served us as well as we served it. Life revolved around the Big Three; General Motors, Chrysler and Ford. Their assembly lines may have been in the Motor City, but it was out-state Michigan and especially Kent County (home to Grand Rapids) that made the parts that supplied the domestic auto industry. Heck, back then it was THE auto industry.

Not only was the world of manufacturing as we knew it collapsing, it was changing. A paradox, I know. How can it collapse and change at the same time? There were survivors. Thankfully because of the Obama administration's auto industry investment package, two of our biggest players survived, GM and Chrysler.

However the problem Michigan faced was still twofold: a lack of education and a lack of jobs. Employment was, and is, a victim of advanced manufacturing's success. You need a degree to get into most jobs in advanced manufacturing. No longer can a high-school dropout or even a high-school graduate walk up to the assembly line and fit in. Manufacturing was no longer as simple as a screwdriver, if it ever was. It is still hands-on, but the brain has to tell the hands what to do. A computer is very much a part of the process every step of the way from concept to design to manufacture to market.

At the same time, advanced manufacturing required far fewer employees. The recession, which became the Long Depression in much of Michigan's manufacturing plants, taught the OEMs (original equipment manufacturers) and the companies that supplied them one thing loud and clear: they could do more with less. And in Michigan less turned out to be much less.

What the business community and economists considered productivity, Michigan saw as a disaster.

Grand Rapids was desperately searching for a new cluster of prosperity. Something had to replace office furniture and the auto supply chain. Kent County, Michigan was once the epicenter for the tool-and-die shops that Detroit's auto industry depended on. That was fading fast as the Medical Mile talk heated up.

Usually new business clusters come out of old clusters, the way the office furniture industry grew out of the collapse of the home furniture industry in Grand Rapids, which grew out of a long list of industries that were launched then, fizzled. Grand Rapids once saw itself as the home of great beer brewing, pre-dating the current plethora of micro-breweries that dot the landscape, urban and suburban.

However sometimes evolution needs a jumpstart. Not exactly an epiphany. More like an unusual event that shakes up a community and starts it, collectively, thinking in a new direction, sharing in a new vision. Grand Rapids' unusual event was the creation of Van Andel Institute.

"I remember very clearly the day I received a call in 1995 from David Van Andel," Birgit Klohs recalled. "I was sitting in my office and was told that two floors down, they would be making this announcement of a private institute being endowed by his parents for the research of cancer diseases."

I sat in the office with my phone held to my ear, ecstatic. My first thought was 'oh, my God, a new industry.' My next thought was 'spinoffs' and my mind starting racing."

An economic developer, like Birgit, markets the strength that an area already has. Life sciences Grand Rapids did not have. For Grand Rapids to be even dreaming of a life sciences cluster seemed like utter foolishness at the time to many. Brigit and the others who had this vision had work to do.

She understood that some may have doubted the vision. "While we had very fine colleges and universities, there was not a research university in this community," she said. History had shown the necessity of a research university. Boston and San Diego have grown bio- and life-science clusters largely because of the educational institutions in, and near, those cities.

"So for a philanthropist to give this incredible gift of a research institute staffed with world-class researchers from at one time 17 countries, and probably more now was a game changer on a lot of different levels," Birgit explained.

That philanthropist was Jay Van Andel, one of the legends of West Michigan. He was not just a self-made millionaire. He was a self-made billionaire. And as was explained in the last chapter, when Jay Van Andel started making real money, he began following the model that had been used to reinvent Grand Rapids and would create the Medical Mile. Those who have money in Grand Rapids, give money to Grand Rapids. He had it. He gave it.

That was only one of the dramas that played out as Medical Mile was created. The other was far more contentious.

The creation of Medical Mile ran parallel to the merger of Butterworth Hospital and Blodgett Medical Center. There were four hospitals in the city at the time. Metro Health would opt out of the Medical Mile, eventually deciding to leave Grand Rapids and build its own health care community in southern Kent County. Saint Mary's Health Care would also decide against moving to Michigan Street NE. It would instead create its own version of Medical Mile, while still being closely connected to the original Mile.

The realignment of Grand Rapids' health care community began with the creation of the Hillman Commission in 1993 to conduct a Special Kent County Area Health Care Facilities Study.

The commission, chaired by U.S. District Judge Douglas W. Hillman, was organized by Alliance for Health and assigned the task of conducting a comprehensive review of hospital plans in Kent County and to make appropriate recommendations for the future. It ultimately provided a far-reaching blueprint for the community that led to the merger of Butterworth and Blodgett and the creation of Spectrum Health Systems, Inc.

The Hillman Commission first asked all of the hospitals to share their plans for the future before releasing its own very specific vision. It recommended that Blodget not take a separate relocation path even though that facility's board had wanted to go to a site on the northeast side of Grand Rapids, outside of what was thought of as the downtown district.

However, that was not the Commission's top priority. The panel recognized that a new focus was needed in the health care community. Job-number one: creating the most critical piece needed to start, and eventually complete, the Medical Mile puzzle.

"The first recommendation of the Hillman Commission was not about relocating Blodgett. It was about strengthening medical education and research," recalled Alliance for Health CEO Lodewyk (Lody) Zwarensteyn, "because those are associated with a high quality of service and that high quality of service is more important than to say, 'Butterworth is on first or Blodgett is on first.'"

Alliance for Health and the Hillman Commission did recommend the hospitals come together rather than Blodgett building a full hospital. "That created the impetus for Spectrum Health. The chairs of the boards of Butterworth and Blodgett, Rich DeVos and Dave Wagner, respectively, got together and agreed that a merger would make a lot of sense," Lody said.

The initial plans were to move the most- intensive health care services downtown, to build off the core that was Butterworth Hospital. "Butterworth was emerging as the winner in the hospital sweepstakes at the time, so they were optioning property up and down Michigan Street for their expansion, with or without Blodgett," said Zwarensteyn. "They were planning an aggressive future on their own."

Putting Blodgett into the new plan changed the dynamic for Butterworth. It radically revised the vision for Michigan Street, which would become the avenue of the life sciences and health care cluster of prosperity.

There were some interesting concepts that were discussed, drafted and rejected. One was the idea of turning Michigan Street into a tunnel, with the health facilities built on top of it in kind of a Silo City.

"Drawings were made that showed towers up and down Michigan

Street, distinct units for different services all up and down Michigan Hill," said Zwarensteyn.

Saint Mary's Health Care CEO Phil McCorkle, who was with Butterworth when the merger and the concept of Medical Mile were first being considered, told me he was the one who facilitated Jay Van Andel's dream of creating Van Andel Institute and then Medical Mile.

Bruce Brown, who had been Indianapolis' city manager, brought McCorkle a different concept. He thought there was a better option than creating this community on Michigan Street. Brown wanted to build Medical Mile in a Silo City over I-196, just like they had done when he worked in Indianapolis.

Neither of those ideas ever went any farther than an architect's rendering. But the planning did lay the groundwork for what would become Medical Mile.

"The concept of having facilities up and down Michigan was in the minds of leaders two decades ago, and gradually through the Butterworth-Blodget merger process, consultants helped bring this about," Phil said.

He also said the land on which the Van Andel Institute, the powerhouse research facility that would anchor the Mile was eventually built, was originally going to be home to a Ronald McDonald House. "There was a concern that Butterworth would have a relationship with the RMD house that was too close, so they decided to put it on a neutral site."

McCorkle was part of the early discussions about bringing Michigan State University's College of Human Medicine to the Mile.

"We were thinking about naming it 'Michigan Mile,' but we were afraid Michigan State University would never want to get close to anything named 'Michigan Mile," said McCorkle.

As anyone from Michigan will tell you, the U-M vs. MSU rivalry is nothing to take lightly, and why wasn't the University of Michigan fighting for a place on Medical Mile? Some of the top educators in Grand Rapids weren't able to answer that question for me.

Be that as it may, Medical Mile was moving closer to becoming Grand Rapids next cluster of prosperity. Spectrum Health Systems was created out of the Butterworth-Blodgett merger. The Van Andel Research Institute was built. Scientists from around the world were working on curing diseases that plagued the world. Discussions began to bring the MSU College of Human Medicine to the Mile.

What could possibly go wrong with that? Grand Rapids could go wrong with that. What lay ahead was an enormous challenge for the city. For the world to think differently of us, we had to begin thinking differently about ourselves.

It began with the creation of Van Andel Institute, a building that seemed very mysterious to a lot of the people in Grand Rapids. What were they really doing in there? And who are all of these people going and out? VAI was attracting people who didn't look like we did, speak like we did, worship like we did or even eat the same food as we did.

The culture shift had begun.

CHAPTER SIX:
Van Andel Institute: The Anchor

GOV. JOHN ENGLER WANTED to build the Michigan Life Sciences Corridor. One of the richest men in the world got Grand Rapids connected to it.

Dave Van Andel was more than an early-backer and developer of Medical Mile. During a conversation with Engler, the CEO of Van Andel Institute proposed the idea of building a corridor linking West Michigan to the Life Sciences Corridor. The goal was to bring researchers at Wayne State University in Detroit, the University of Michigan in Ann Arbor and Medical Mile in Grand Rapids into a partnership that would create a trinity that would be on the scale of clusters on the east and west coasts of the U.S.

Grand Rapids is never going to become a mega-city on its own, at least not in our lifetime. However most economic developers believe it is the "mega-cities" like Boston, Chicago, New York, etc. that will be the hubs of innovation and really the hubs of life in the near future. So what's a city like Grand Rapids to do? Find partnerships and create the scale it takes to compete. Chalk that up as another valuable lesson.

There is also a lot to learn about the leverage it took to bring Grand Rapids into this life sciences cluster. The city was not thought of as being part of that community any more than the city thought of itself as being a health care community.

How did it happen? How did the ugly girl get a date for the prom? It is important to remember this was more than just a suggestion from a constituent. It came from a very active Republican family of billionaires. Dave's father and Rich DeVos learned early on that those with money had to give money if they were to have influence in the GOP. Engler was a lifelong Republican.

So, Grand Rapids became part Gov. Engler's Michigan Life Sciences

Corridor concept. This opened the tap of state and federal money. It poured in. Aid from Washington and Lansing helped build the Corridor and Medical Mile. This is another valuable lesson to be remembered when it comes time to build the next cluster of prosperity: The Medical Mile could not have been built without the minds and money of Grand Rapids. Washington's and Lansing's assistance was also invaluable. Smart government is very much a partner that needs to be invited to the table.

The Governor who followed Engler, Jennifer Granholm, turned the Life Sciences Corridor into the Michigan Technology Tri-Corridor, expanding the initiative to include advanced manufacturing, homeland security and life sciences research. It then became one massive economic development effort that could use part of Michigan's share of the federal government's settlement with the nation's tobacco companies to pay for expansion.

Money was, is, and will always be critical to the Medical Mile. But don't forget about the shared visions of opportunity and impending doom. Anyone who sells advertising will tell you nothing motivates like the fear of loss. Michigan was about to hit this iceberg we came to call the "Great Recession," John Engler and Dave Van Andel had the foresight to see that they could do more than rearrange the deck chairs. They had a chance to build a new boat. But what they did was even more than that.

"We have it within our power to begin the world all over again," wrote Thomas Paine in Common Sense. That comes very close to what Van Andel, DeVos, and the rest were doing with the Medical Mile.

Engler, Van Andel and Birgit Klohs wanted us to re-invent the community by re-inventing the way we thought about ourselves. They knew we needed to create a new generation of entrepreneurs, community leaders and philanthropists, something that could not be done without a new mindset, a new view of ourselves as being part of the bigger global community.

But first, we had to create a "place" for all of that to happen. That is what they did on Michigan Street NE.

The Michigan Life Sciences Corridor that morphed into the Tri-Technologies Corridor helped to create a linkage between three of the key players on Medical Mile: VAI, Michigan State University and Grand Valley State University, along with a life sciences research connection (and competition) between the Grand Rapids entities, Wayne State University in Detroit and the University of Michigan in Ann Arbor.

Dave said, "We (he and Gov. Engler) had the conversation, and then he came back to me and said "you know I want to do this." Engler even signed the legislation to create the Michigan Life Sciences Corridor in the unfinished building that became VAI with Dave standing at his side.

Van Andel remembered making the call to Birgit to he told her what was going to happen. "I don't think anybody realized at the time, including myself perhaps, how big a deal this really was," Dave said in his very comfortable way.

"You have to understand that back then, if you were having a discussion about life sciences in Michigan, people would look at you funny and go, "what?"

Looking back on it, I can remember being one those people asking that single word and maybe simple-minded question. What? Writing some of the first stories about Medical Mile for a regional business publication I was left wondering if I should use the phrase "life science" or "life sciences." We were all wondering if there was more to a "wet lab" than a sink and running water. Dave Van Andel was truly opening the door to a new world for Grand Rapids.

To tell you the truth, I thought they were nuts. That was a mistake. It was also a lesson for the developers of the next cluster: there will be non-believers. Anything worth doing is worth doubting. In fact, that should be encouraged. There is nothing wrong with critical thinking.

However, the early adopters had to be patient.

"This wasn't automotive technology, this wasn't anything to do with furniture, this was life sciences and this was something that was certainly not on the radar screen and certainly was not in the vocabulary of 99 percent of the populace," Dave said.

"When I made the call to tell her (Birgit) what was going to occur now, what the decision was, what this meant, I think that was an inflection point, if you will, that quite frankly changed the conversation forever about what Grand Rapids was going to become."

No kidding.

"I also remember a call from then-Mayor (John) Logie who asked 'what does this mean?'" recalled Birgit. "I remember John asking, 'what's a spin off?' 'It is really when someone has an innovation that becomes a full-fledged business over time,' I explained."

She explained to him and everyone else whose world had been shaken and whose minds were soon to be opened to unthinkable possibilities that first of all it meant that Grand Rapids was going to have to attract "incredible intellectual capacity."

Intellect does attract intellect, and talent attracts talent. After the

Detroit Tigers had the worst season in baseball history, owner Mike Illitch recruited and signed a real all-star, Ivan "Pudge" Rodriguez to the team, and then used Pudge to recruit and attract other top talent.

The same thing is happening on Medical Mile, just as Birgit predicted more than a decade ago.

She knew that the walls of a research institute of this magnitude would have to be papered with lots of framed Ph.D. diplomas. There would be many other support positions, as well. But the core of that institute would be Ph.D. scientists.

"And from that I told people, you will hopefully get spin-offs, you will get clinical trials, and we are going to have to talk venture capital," explained Birgit. I could see in her eyes 15 years after that phone call that her mind must have been spinning when all this happened. Even now she gets more and more excited recalling the early days of Medical Mile conversations. It is hard not to get caught up in the enthusiasm.

"Eventually somebody is going to invent something, or find something or a cure for something that will turn into a business," said Birgit. That has always been the dream, the vision, the hope, that someone, some day would create the next "sticky notes" of life sciences and move Grand Rapids off the average plate.

It is happening now on Medical Mile. We will look at progress made in later chapters. However during the creation days Grand Rapids had to, and is still, learning a new vocabulary.

Van Andel Institute, this anchor of the Medical Mile, was not only a game changer; it was an attitude- and vision-changer for metro Grand Rapids.

Birgit can forgive us for being confused in the days that followed the phone call from Dave. She was too.

"What we said to the Right Place board was, 'We are getting this incredible gift. We don't particularly know what it means. But let's figure out what we need to put around it to make it worthwhile.'"

To accomplish that, RPI commissioned a Deloitte & Touche study. It showed metro Grand Rapids would need venture capital, wet lab space, incubators and more.

The unintended consequence or perhaps the unknown consequence of the Van Andel Institute was really what has happened off the Medical Mile. Here is another lesson for the next cluster creators: whatever you do is going to impact not only your cluster but the entire community.

"I compare it to the creation of Grand Valley State University 50 years ago," said Birgit. "There was a small group of people who wanted their own university in Grand Rapids. It was the second-biggest community in the state (of Michigan) and we didn't have our own university."

"They plopped the university, at the time Grand Valley State College, in the middle of Ottawa County and started with 200 or 300 students. Today it is the fastest growing university with a major campus downtown, a major campus in Allendale, masters' degree programs. It has become a huge economic generator in our region. It figures in everything we do."

The people who turned Grand Valley State College into a university have also made it a driving force in the new Grand Rapids. It plays a major role on Medical Mile with the Cook-DeVos Center for Health Sciences and I believe it has been the top force in reshaping downtown Grand Rapids into what former Gov. Jennifer Granholm urged us to make it, a "Cool City," attracting and retaining the post-Boomer generations.

This was not an economic development model of creative destruction. GVSU did it without breaking anything we had on the shelf in downtown Grand Rapids. They just added things to make it better.

The same thing is happening with Medical Mile. Grand Rapids is still heavily involved in supplying the automotive industry. Office furniture manufacturing might have been scaled back and down, as has the auto industry involvement, but both are still here.

And as I was writing *Last Chance Mile*, I was also working on a series of articles focusing on a new problem faced by manufacturing; a lack of talent. It could be that some of the lessons we are learning on the Medical Mile will help us build a Manufacturing Mile. Who knows?

Whatever the future may hold, this is not the Grand Rapids I moved into in 1990. The shift started even before ground was broken for Van Andel Institute. But when earth was turned for the VAI on Michigan Street the pace of innovation certainly changed.

"Now all of a sudden we have added a new dimension, this thing called life sciences," Dave told me. "We knew back then it had great potential but really had no idea what it would become."

The arms of construction cranes filled the skies like the metallic limbs of H.G. Wells' invaders in The War of the Worlds. Cement was poured, foundations laid, politicians told us it was a "great day to be in Grand Rapids," the city that was described as the shining jewel of Michigan.

The cranes were creating what we all hoped would be a cluster of prosperity at a time when the rest of Michigan, the Great Lakes region and the Midwest were all standing on the Rust Belt sidelines, watching Grand Rapids grow.

But then the cranes were gone. Construction stopped. The buildings were done. A local TV station reported that development on Medical Mile had stalled.

Nothing could have been further from the truth and that was really the motivation for writing this book.

When I told Birgit about the TV station's take on the cranes disappearing from Grand Rapids' skyline, she was outraged.

"Look at the talent that these institutions, VAI, Spectrum, Saint Mary's, MSU and GVSU, are now attracting," said Klohs. "What people don't realize is the interconnectivity between those five institutions. Sometimes it might seem more competitive, but MSU and Saint Mary's have jointly hired people. MSU and VAI are doing co-hiring of certain specialists. The same is true for Spectrum and MSU."

Birgit also believes the interconnectivity, particularly between the intellectual talents on the Mile is enormous. "It is like building a very strong web so that one plus one makes three rather than two."

The richness of the Medical Mile lies in the interconnectivity of all of the institutions. "If they were stood alone they would be silos," she said. "You will not attract an urologist, an MD, or a Ph.D., if he or she does not also have an opportunity for an appointment to the medical school, let's just say, and vice versa."

The Medical Mile's majesty is ultimately in the partnerships, the connections and the connectivity between the individual researchers and institutions. That is what makes all boats rise in this cluster of prosperity. And that is why Medical Mile is the real hero of this story.

CHAPTER SEVEN:
Michigan Street: The Hero

THE 1960S WERE A time of reinvention and near-revolution for Grand Rapids just as those years were for the rest of the world. But it was also a decade of tremendous economic growth in Grand Rapids. One of three people, mostly men of course, earned their paychecks in factories. Metal fabricators employed the most; 47-thousand in 1960. Furniture: 7,500.

Capital expenditures by Grand Rapids area companies grew from $25 million in 1963, to $67 million in 1967, to $165 million in 1969. Of course, it was all destined to come crashing down, but these were the glory days for heavy metal and the men who used it to make our cars, trucks, chairs and desks.

The 1960s also gave rise to a new economic development trend in Grand Rapids, industrial parks. What a great idea. There was a lot of vacant land or underutilized acreage in Grand Rapids and the cities that would become its suburbs; especially in Wyoming, Kentwood and Walker. A lot of it was being used by farmers, but let's face it, manufacturing ruled the day. The American agrarian society was on its way out. The culture of Grand Rapids was being reinvented.

One of the most impressive of these developments was a $2.8 million, 360-acre industrial park that included a street named for Roger B. Chaffee. The Grand Rapids man was one of the three astronauts that died in that terrible Gemini space capsule fire.

How expensive and large that park must have seemed at the time. Not much compared to the money invested on the billion-dollar campus that is the Medical Mile, but you have to remember how little people were spending for a pack of cigarettes and a gallon of gasoline back then. It was a different time, and a different world.

The 1960s also saw the rise of shopping centers in metro Grand Rapids. Sometimes the simplest ideas are the best ideas. Put several stores together. Build big lots for free parking, and wait for the people to come. The new shopping centers, and the Woodland Mall, would clear retail out of downtown Grand Rapids, moving the city's biggest stores to the neighborhoods where everyone was living.

More Baby Boomers were entering the world, kicking and squalling, to fill the cribs in those bedroom communities. That meant the Big Four hospitals- Butterworth, Blodgett, St. Mary's and Grand Rapids Osteopathic, soon to become Metropolitan Hospital—had to expand. They were serving 70-thousand patients a year and had 1,400 beds by the middle of the decade.[7]

Butterworth Hospital, which was fated to merge with Blodgett to create Spectrum Health, was the most active business on Michigan Street. Besides the expansion and building going on there, life pretty much went along as it always had in the northeast side neighborhood that had grown up between the St. Isidore Catholic and Immanuel Lutheran churches.

Grand Rapids and its suburbs learned a valuable lesson in the 1960s. Infrastructure wins. None of the shopping malls or industrial parks that changed our landscape could have gone up without power lines for electricity, concrete for the cars or pipes for the water and sewage. You have to have roads, sewers, water, electricity, and natural gas. Nothing happens if that is not in place.

The Medical Mile could not have been successful without all of the above either, and the 21st century infrastructure needed to carry the gases that scientists, researchers and physicians need, along with the fiber-optic pipes needed to transmit all of their information. That is the infrastructure of the future that will have to be constructed for the next cluster of prosperity.

We didn't use the phrase then, but the shopping malls, strip centers, and industrial parks that went up while the U.S. was racing to the Moon and trying to figure out what went wrong in Vietnam were that decade's clusters of prosperity, centered on main thoroughfares like 28th Street in Wyoming, one of the suburbs that stole Grand Rapids' retail luster away. That's where money was changing hands as union shops boomed and manufacturing roared. 28th Street was that decade's Grand River.

---

7   Gordon L. Olson, *Grand Rapids A City Renewed*, (Grand Rapids: Grand Rapids Historical Commission, 1996) 24-25

Grand Rapids would soon learn that Michigan Street is to Medical Mile what 28th Street was to retail and the Grand River was to the Grand Rapids furniture industry. Without the former, the latter could not, and would not, have existed.

Here's the big difference between Medical Mile, 28th Street and the Grand River. The Mile also needed philanthropy. It needed people with money who were willing to give money.

The Michigan Street boom wouldn't happen for another three decades, but it finally would thanks to the philanthropic mindset of one of the richest men in the world in the 1990s.

When Jay Van Andel signed that $1 billion check to get Van Andel Institute started it was a transformative event that opened the philanthropic gates in Grand Rapids allowing millions upon millions of dollars to flow to what would become Medical Mile.

Van Andel, Rich and Helen DeVos, Peter Secchia, Peter Cook, played key roles in creating this Grand Rapids lifeline, helping West Michigan build for the future. And, that is just the beginning of the list of the people who have played a role over the past 15 years in building the Mile.

But I don't believe any of them will prove to be the real star or stars of this story. The real protagonist is the Medical Mile itself, and beyond that Michigan Street NE. Without Michigan Street NE, the home of a $1.5 billion straight line that will hopefully become a concentric circle around the globe, this scientific community could not have been born.

People who are on Michigan Street every day told me that the concrete thoroughfare itself has been the key driver in getting the best talent to drop what it was doing in other parts of the world and move to Grand Rapids. Dr. Patrik Brundin, who moved from Sweden to West Michigan to lead the VAI Parkinson's Disease research effort, is but one example.

But still, bringing people to the Mile has not been easy.

MSU College of Human Medicine Dean Marsha Rappley told me she has had a tough time recruiting people to the Mile. But once they get here, they often stay here. "They are very taken with the quality of life, along with the excellence of the research, the education or the clinical service," she said.

"The institutions of this city are known to be of the highest quality and very high efficiency," Rappley continued. "The people of this community really embrace those institutions. And that is a very strong message for people who may be doing small, focused research. They still want to be part of the bigger whole and that gives them energy to do their work."

She was as astonished as Birgit Klohs was when I repeated the local TV station's story that said development on the Mile had stalled. The reporter also did more than imply the Medical Mile had been a disappointment.

The second phase of the Mile's evolution is taking place inside the buildings that line Michigan Street as the "programmatic pieces" are being put into place, according to Dean Rappley. "Those are the people, the life blood, and the blood and guts of all of the buildings."

It is a very exciting environment. Anyone who walks here on the street or comes to visit can feel the energy," Rappley said. "It was very dramatic when we had all of the cranes in the air. But now it is even more amazing because it is all up and running. When you look at all of the things that have happened the past two years, you have to realize this is pretty phenomenal."

This is a cluster of prosperity and energy. The Medical Mile has become its own community on the banks of Michigan Street just as the shopping centers and retail community grew along 28th Street and the furniture industry was built along the banks of the Grand River.

You couldn't drive down Michigan Street when Medical Mile was being built. Construction crews and their equipment were everywhere.

On the east end of Medical Mile, they put up the GVSU Cook-DeVos Center for Health Sciences, the home of Grand Valley State University's Allied Health Professions programs. It is also the home of the West Michigan Science and Technology Initiative where new life sciences and medical device businesses are being slowly and painfully birthed for this community, on those lab benches.

Spectrum-Butterworth Hospital is unrecognizable today, compared to what it was when it was just known as Butterworth Hospital. Helen DeVos Children's Hospital has been created adjacent to the expanded Spectrum-Butterworth facility, filling the Medical Mile skyline, a giant blue building unlike anything ever seen in Grand Rapids.

A Burger King restaurant was flattened to make room for Spectrum Health's Lemmen-Holton Cancer Pavilion on the northern shoulders of Michigan Street, across from Spectrum-Butterworth and DeVos Children's hospitals.

The Meijer Heart Center was built from the ground up creating a facility that attracted some of the world's best heart specialists who would perform the first heart transplants in Grand Rapids. That is something that was totally unthinkable 15 years ago.

Michigan State University College of Human Medicine anchors the west end of the Mile, attracting the next generation of doctors, and those who will lead them. On the south side of the Mile, right across the street from MSU is the Van Andel Research Institute.

All of this is so new, so modern, creating so much new energy in Grand Rapids. From the Cook-DeVos Center for Health Sciences to Spectrum-Butterworth to Michigan State University's College of Human Medicine and of course to Van Andel Institute, it is a brave, new world for Grand Rapids.

But stuck at the west end of all of this action like the typographical error an editor couldn't find is Immanuel Lutheran Church. This last remaining evidence of what Grand Rapids was two centuries ago can be seen from the MSU College of Human Medicine plaza. It looks like the church is being swallowed whole by the Mile. It is as out of place as a pair of brown shoes in a tuxedo store's front window.

The West Michigan Science and Technology Initiative needs to be on Medical Mile. It is right where it should be. Venture Center Director Rich Cook, whose office is on the top floor of the Cook-DeVos Center of Health Sciences at Michigan and Lafayette, gets very excited talking about the Michigan Street- Grand River analogy.

Remember how important it is to create a community for talent?

"We have an unusual confluence of three institutions within five to seven minutes of walking distance," Cook explained. "We have VAI, which is a major research institute, Spectrum-Butterworth, which is a teaching hospital and the MSU College of Human Medicine."

So, as he explained it, a physician can walk from the bedside of a patient at Spectrum-Butterworth and go down the street, just a couple of city blocks, to Van Andel Research Institute if that patient is involved in a clinical trial. Then, he or she could walk over to MSU to teach a class.

"The ability to walk five to seven minutes to get where you want to go without getting in a car is what is powering these jobs," Cook said. "When I came here in February of '07 there were 4,000 people working on Medical Mile. Last year (2010) there were 7,000 and that is likely to grow to 8,000. That is all the result of these institutions being so close to each other."

Birgit Klohs said it would be a billion-dollar campus if it wasn't for Michigan Street. "It is a billion-dollar campus," said Rich gesturing with the plastic spoon he was using to eat breakfast from a McDonald's parfait cup. "The road doesn't divide it. The road connects it."

"We pulled people here from NIH (National Institutes of Health) because they didn't have to park away from a campus and ride 40 minutes in a shuttle bus to get to their offices," said Rich. "Here they can drive down Michigan, park right under their building and walk into work."

Just as the Grand River brought logs to the furniture companies, Michigan Street brings information and the world to the students, teachers, doctors, researchers, scientists and technicians who are working on the Medical Mile.

"It is the right-of-way for the major pipe we have for fiber optics," said Rich. "It is huge and is constantly busy moving patient records, the business plans of entrepreneurs, and our data to Van Andel (Research Institute). You can't do this work without a strong Internet."

"Were we on a campus with all of these institutions together on a piece of green land, doctors would not be able to park close and we would not have as strong an Internet system," he said. "It used to be rivers and now it is roads, fiber optics and pipes delivering gases."

When Spectrum Health put in additional electrical capacity there were multiple pipes under the ground to carry it. And now, Spectrum, Grand Valley State University and Michigan State University are buying up more property on the Mile. The infrastructure under Michigan Street supports that.

Rich added his voice to those who disagreed with the TV station's report that said development had stalled on Michigan Street. The news report also said that some people who had move to Grand Rapids from Chicago were unhappy that they had not found another Chicago.

"People like to justify their existence by saying things are not good, but frankly this is one of the best things in Michigan right now," he told me. "Grand Rapids is seen as a leader in growing jobs."

Like Dean Rappley and Birgit Klohs, Cook also pointed out that the Medical Mile has served as a magnet to keep students in Grand Rapids. "Students who have an under-grad degree in bio technology or cellular molecular biology, and masters' program students get pipelined into Van Andel Institute and MSU. The Mile on Michigan Street helps them too," according to Cook. "They intern for a while, they can walk down, they can walk back, they can get hired permanently and then they have a good paying job and they can stay here."

The Medical Mile could not have happened without the mile that is Michigan Street. The institutions are not just connected geographically. It is a mindset, a cluster of prosperity mentality that goes beyond the shopping centers or industrial parks of the 20th century.

The Parkinson's disease research that is happening in Grand Rapids is happening on the Medical Mile because of that campus and cluster mentality. This research brings together competing organizations like Saint Mary's Health Care and Spectrum Health along with the Michigan State University College of Human Medicine and Van Andel Institute.

It is another shared vision on Medical Mile and another example of individual insight becoming collective insight. The overriding idea of what drives the Mile is the concept that the institutions on the backbone of Michigan Street NE are accomplishing more together than they could ever dream of doing alone.

CHAPTER EIGHT:
The Parkinson's Partnership

WHEN GRAND RAPIDS RECOGNIZES a problem, Grand Rapids takes action.

Sanitation was nearly non-existent in the early 1900s. Open garbage wagons were common on the streets of Grand Rapids. People routinely threw trash and food into their backyards where roaming animals, packs of dogs, or the family pigs would eat it.

But as Grand Rapids' population grew, there were too many families producing too much garbage and too few animals to eat it.

As we learned earlier, that led to the establishment of "piggeries" a cluster of prosperity if you will, in which herds of pigs would eat garbage collected by "scavengers" who were earning 25-cents per house in 1905. The piggery concept didn't last long. Even pigs can only eat so much, and a pig is what a pig eats. If it has been eating garbage, you know what the pork from that animal is going to taste like. There was also one documented case of pigs eating peaches that had been thrown away after being pickled in alcohol. They were what they ate. The pigs collapsed, too drunk to stand.[8]

Here was another lesson to be learned and remembered: Not every cluster of prosperity is going to last. That is why the Medical Mile cannot stand still and why Grand Rapids has to be driving the next opportunity, the next cluster of prosperity.

No one worried about littering in those days. Everyone just did it. And spitting? Every man who chewed tobacco, and there were few who did not, felt free to let a long stream of tobacco juice fly when needed.

All of that spitting and littering and open garbage let to thousands of

---

8   Z.Z. Lydens, editor, *The Story of Grand Rapids*, (Grand Rapids: Kregel Publications, 1966) 200-201

flies. The insects were everywhere there were people in Grand Rapids, and along with flies, came disease. Flies were such a problem in the homes of Grand Rapidians that a new business was created to manufacture a brand of flypaper called Tanglefoot. Ribbons of the sticky paper were hung in Grand Rapids homes for years after the turn of the 20th century.[9]

But still families battled flies "that swarmed by the hundreds" at supper time, using whatever was at hand to chase the insects out of their kitchens that usually doubled as dining rooms.

Anti-fly crusades were very popular in Grand Rapids. The Grand Rapids Press and The Grand Rapids News reporter and editor, Z.Z. Lydens noted in his book "The Story of Grand Rapids" that school children killed more than 16,000 of the insects in 1912.[10]

The school kids' fly-killing contest was part of Grand Rapids' pioneering efforts against a disease that was killing people across America, tuberculosis. Foreshadowing what would happen less than 100 years later, the Grand Rapids Anti-Tuberculosis Society set up a "preventorium" in 1919 on the street that would become the Mile. More than 40 children, who came from TB-exposed homes that had been quarantined by Kent County health officials, were sheltered there.

The Anti-Tuberculosis Society, the first of its kind in Michigan, hired a visiting nurse in 1905 to help care for TB patients in their homes, and three years later opened a tuberculosis clinic that was staffed by six doctors.

The Society also established a sanatorium for TB patients in Sunshine Hospital on Fuller Avenue, less than two miles from where Medical Mile would be built. The name of that institution serves as more than a clue of what they were planning to do.[11]

Sunshine physicians investigated the use of "open air treatment" for their patients. The Grand Rapids schools experimented with "open air" school classrooms, while the Society also worked to win approval of an "anti-spitting" ordinance as part of the battle against TB.

We have come a long way from anti-spitting ordinances and Sunshine Hospital with its open-air treatment of TB patients. But, that legacy still holds a valuable lesson that led to the creation of the Medical Mile; Grand

---

9   Z.Z. Lydens, editor, *The Story of Grand Rapids*, (Grand Rapids: Kregel Publications, 1966),

10   Z.Z. Lydens, editor, *The Story of Grand Rapids*, (Grand Rapids: Kregel Publications, 1966), 376-377

11   Z.Z. Lydens, editor, *The Story of Grand Rapids*, (Grand Rapids: Kregel Publications, 1966), 390-391

Rapids' spirit of collaboration and partnership has to be a part of anything that is going to last.

That attitude led the efforts to make the city a better place in the past, and it is the shared vision that is leading the evolution of the Mile as institutions that are really competing for West Michigan's health care business are also collaborating to battle diseases plaguing humanity.

Parkinson's disease is the target of one of those unified efforts. Parkinson's is a chronic and progressive movement disorder that afflicts an estimated seven to 10 million people worldwide, according to the Parkinson's disease Foundation. That includes more than one million Americans who are living with the disease, more than the combined number of people diagnosed with multiple sclerosis, muscular dystrophy and Lou Gehrig's disease.

Ever meet someone with whom you have something in common that seems to create an immediate connection?

That had to have happened when Dave Van Andel and Patrik Brundin, M.D., Ph.D met. The electricity must have been tremendous.

Both of their fathers were born in 1924 and both of their fathers died of Parkinson's. We fast forward to 2011. That is when Dave Van Andel and Patrik Brundin teamed up to do something about Parkinson's in the institution that Dave's father created.

Dr. Brundin is an internationally renowned expert in the field of Parkinson's and neurodegenerative disease research, who coordinates multi-disciplinary networks. He has been one of the most cited researchers in the field of neuroscience in the past 20 years.

Grand Rapids got him. As Marsha Rappley, Rich Cook and Birgit Klohs have already pointed out, this would not have happened without Medical Mile, which could not have happened anywhere but Michigan Street NE.

While Brundin was in Sweden building his part of the foundation for what was to become an historic alliance on Medical Mile, The Jay Van Andel Parkinson Research Lab was being created in Grand Rapids.

Dr. Patrik Brundin has been called, "a rock star in his field" but you would never know it by looking at him. Brundin is a thin, wiry man whose brainpower could light a city. He told the Medical Mile Resource Group at the Medical Mile's Van Andel Research Institute in March 2012 that there is new hope in the quest to cure people afflicted with Alzheimer's and Parkinson's diseases.

Brundin also said, in his very European, smooth, cultured way, that he is finding smaller institutions like VARI are doing a much better job in this endeavor than their larger counterparts in Big Pharma.

"Very few drugs are being developed because (the process) is so difficult and expensive," said Dr. Brundin. "The drug industry is on the brink of giving up."

But Dr. Brundin is not. He recently brought his family across an ocean, settling them in a city that they never heard of to join the Van Andel Institute's fight against Parkinson's, Alzheimer's and other brain diseases.

There is a long way to go. We can be no more certain of victory against these burdens on our world than the British could be sure of survival when Winston Churchill flashed the famous "V" for victory sign and vowed to press on, as London was being bombed.

Dr. Brundin was honest with his audience, telling them that "the disease process cannot be stopped. Less than 10 percent of new drugs work (against brain diseases). Current therapies are unsatisfactory."

However he added there is "great hope" in "tricking stem cells" into becoming dopamine neurons, and that could open the door to, if not cures, at least a way to slow or inhibit the spread of Parkinson's and Alzheimer's.

The best hope could be found in research institutions like the VARI on Grand Rapids' Medical Mile, or as Dr. Brundin put it, "small may be beautiful." He said their rate of success is much higher than Big Pharma is seeing, and the cost of research and discovery is far lower.

Why? That is another mystery that is yet to be solved. But it could be because Big Pharma may not have, in Brundin's words, "the right creative culture."

We are hoping the "right, creative culture" is the 'high on thought, low on bureaucracy attitude' that is found on the Medical Mile. Brundin said it could even be "serendipitous," although he said that his team has a different definition for that word.

Rather than making great discoveries by serendipitous accident, Brundin said, with a smile on his face, "We prefer to see it as a happy blend of wisdom and luck." Then he bounced out the door. The Medical Mile Resource Group (of which I am a member) wanted to ask questions. But Brundin was already back in his room of science.

Dr. Brundin was appointed the inaugural holder of the Jay Van Andel Endowed Chair in Parkinson's Research, in October 2011, a development that was, "a crucial piece in our fight against this terrible disease. With his recruitment, our initiative in this area is going to a whole new level," Dave Van Andel said during a recording session for the WOOD Radio "Clearly Community" program that I hosted.

This battle against diseases plaguing humanity is another example of those with money giving some of that money to Grand Rapids. It is also a case of relationships and friendships that last for decades. Endowed by generous gifts from Richard and Helen DeVos, each of their four children, and the Frey Foundation, Brundin's laboratory was opened in Van Andel Institute's Phase II, a 240-thousand-square-foot, $178 million expansion in late 2009.

Van Andel also told me that the expansion into Parkinson's and other neurodegenerative diseases like ALS and Alzheimer's should not have come as a surprise to anyone who has been following the Mile. When VAI opened it had a focus on cancer.

"We knew we were going to branch out from cancer at some point. The only question was when. I think the exciting thing is that we are doing this only 11 years later. We didn't think we would be able to do it, this quickly."

It is also an exciting development for those who had been watching the development and evolution of this grand experiment known as Medical Mile for more than 15 years. Many of us in Grand Rapids believe the recruitment of Dr. Brundin has put the Mile on a new level in the research community.

A press release issued by Van Andel Institute to announce the Brundin appointment expressed that very well, describing it as the "latest in a series of research and clinical developments all within blocks of one another on Medical Mile, which situates West Michigan as a potential leader in basic and translational Parkinson's research."[12]

It was also the latest in a series of collaborative partnerships that grew the Mile into something that could become the "concentric circle around the globe," that VAI VP Jerry Callahan mentioned during an interview for this book. That is a concept that person after person on the Mile has applauded.

Brundin's appointment was not the first foray into Parkinson's research on Medical Mile. And while his recruitment was not a case of Medical Mile's gain at someone else' loss – his lab known as the Neuronal Survival

---

12   Van Andel Institute Press Release, *Van Andel Institute Appoints Dr. Patrik Brundin*, Oct. 27, 2011

Unit will be maintained at Lund University in Sweden – the Mile's entry into Parkinson's research does involve the recruitment of other researchers who moved their operations into Grand Rapids.

Michigan State University recruited a team of Parkinson's disease researchers from the University of Cincinnati in 2009. They brought with them a $6.2 million Morris K. Udall Center of Excellence in Parkinson's disease Research Grant that was awarded by the National Institutes of Health.

"This is what we all hoped would happen. It is actually beyond what we thought we would see in the first few years. It has just happened like that," MSU College of Human Medicine Dean Marsha Rappley said, snapping her fingers.

She described the four principal investigators on the Udall Research team as "amazing, very high quality people. As individuals, they are very much about building and creating opportunity for other people. It is not just about how wonderful their research is. It is also about the opportunity they are creating for other people."

"There is a selfless quality about these people as individuals that has attracted many others, including Dr. Brundin and others who are more junior in their careers," said Rappley.

So this is another lesson that we can learn from the Medical Mile and transfer to the next cluster of prosperity in Grand Rapids: As has been noted before, talent attracts talent. And now we learn that the best talent should always be worried about growing a new generation to follow themselves.

This really came as a bombshell of optimism for Grand Rapids. These MSU –formerly University of Cincinnati –researchers, whose labs are now within the confines of VAI and on the expanse of Medical Mile, have the opportunity to collaborate with Brundin's team to develop a world-class Parkinson's disease enterprise spanning basic, translational and clinical research.

That was not the only development that caught Grand Rapids' attention in 2011.

This is also an example of the scope of Medical Mile. This research community is not limited to Michigan Street NE. Saint Mary's Health Care opened the Hauenstein Center, treating Parkinson's patients along with providing a list of additional neuroscience services.

This is indicative of a key Medical Mile linkage. Not only do we find researchers and investigators on Medical Mile, we also find specialists and patients for clinical trials only blocks away.

Then there is the money. And yes, that is another lesson that needs to be remembered as Grand Rapids builds its next cluster of prosperity: We need to keep growing our next generation of philanthropists, remembering that the giving will have to be much more multi-lateral and inclusive.

Some money is already coming to Medical Mile from outside Grand Rapids. The Michael J. Fox Foundation for Parkinson's Research announced an award of $400,000 to Michigan State University and Van Andel Research Institute in July 2011 for an investigation of the drug Fasudil that has the potential to not only alleviate Parkinson's symptoms, but to actually halt the disease's progress.

"Who would have thought 10 years ago that the community would get a $400,000 grant from Michael J. Fox to do this?" said The Right Place President Birgit Klohs. "Who would have thought we would have been able to attract someone like a Jack Lipton who brought an incredible research team of 24 Ph.Ds. who move en masse from Cincinnati to Grand Rapids. He is one of the foremost Parkinson's researchers."

"There would have been no way to attract someone like Jack Lipton to Grand Rapids 16 years ago," she said. "Attract him to what?"

Recruiting top-level talent to Medical Mile has been a challenge, as we have documented. However, no one on the Mile is shy about inviting the best and brightest from around the world to see what Grand Rapids has to offer.

More than 800 Parkinson's patients and their caregivers came to Grand Rapids in August 2011 for the Davis Phinney Foundation's Victory Summit, giving them an opportunity to meet with the leading Parkinson's researchers and investigators, exchange information, and of course see –and be sold on—Grand Rapids, which is another key component of the recruitment of new talent and patients for Medical Mile.

The importance of the patients, whether they are being treated for cancer, Parkinson's, ALS or Alzheimer's should not be underestimated. The researchers have to have them for clinical trials, and the Mile needs the revenue that is generated by their treatment. Bringing in those new health care dollars is the best way to ultimately lower the cost of health care for West Michigan.

The Mile has to have top-level talent, like Dr. Brundin, to make the rest of it possible. That is why Dave Van Andel told us during that "Clearly Community" recording session that he worked so hard, for more than a year, to make it happen.

Dave had obstacles to overcome. He had to convince Brundin that he could further his research on Medical Mile in a way that he could not in Sweden. Dave also had to convince Brundin and his wife, another top mind in research, that Grand Rapids would be a community in which they could make a new home for themselves.

Talent is attracted by talent, but talent needs more than a lab, talent needs a community. Now we see that we must attach another sentence to the lesson: Talent often has a family.

The wife: Dr. Lena Brundin. She was the "trailing spouse," and any recruiter will tell you they can't close the deal without finding a place for that person. Grand Rapids nearly lost a major hospital executive who moved to West Michigan from Iowa in 1990, because his wife looked around and said, "I am not staying here. This isn't even Des Moines."

Fortunately this is not the Grand Rapids she, or I, moved into in 1990, any more.

Dr. Lena Brundin, an accomplished researcher and associate professor of Experimental Psychiatry at Lund University –just imagine the brainpower in their home that includes three children and a Spanish Water Dog—has accepted an appointment at the Michigan State University College of Human Medicine in the Department of Translational Science and Molecular Medicine. She will be working on the Medical Mile.

So that was one hurdle cleared. The "trailing spouse" is accounted for. But, Grand Rapids' reputation can be a problem. It gets so cold here in the winter, right?

In this case, "the good news as far as Brundin is concerned," Dave said, "is that moving to West Michigan from Sweden is like moving to Hawaii. It is a much warmer climate."

But seriously, folks…it took several discussions and a lot of negotiation to get Brundin to Medical Mile.

"The biggest thing was to get him here, to show him the facilities, to show him the opportunities, and people like Brundin understand this is a huge opportunity to advance their research, and impact even a broader spectrum."

"It takes a lot of time, a lot of talking back and forth and eventually you get to a 'yes,'" Van Andel told me. "And I have found that getting to the "yes" is very often helped by the Medical Mile itself."

As this book went to press, a new story broke regarding the payoff of this investment, this collaboration on Medical Mile. Well, let me back up. It did not happen on the geographic Medical Mile that is limited by the boundaries of College and Division avenues on Michigan Street NE. It took place on the Medical Mile that is a concentric circle around the globe. The word came to Grand Rapids from Van Andel Research Institute April 19, 2012:

"Researchers at Lund University in Sweden have discovered a new stem cell in the adult brain. These cells can proliferate and form several different cell types - most importantly, they can form new brain cells. Scientists hope to take advantage of the finding to develop methods to heal and repair disease and injury in the brain.

Analyzing brain tissue from biopsies, the researchers for the first time found stem cells located around small blood vessels in the brain. The cell's specific function is still unclear, but its plastic properties suggest great potential.

"A similar cell type has been identified in several other organs where it can promote regeneration of muscle, bone, cartilage and adipose tissue," said Patrik Brundin, M.D., Ph.D., Jay Van Andel Endowed Chair in Parkinson's Research at Van Andel Research Institute (VARI), Head of the Neuronal Survival Unit at Lund University and senior author of the study.

In other organs, researchers have shown clear evidence that these types of cells contribute to repair and wound healing. Scientists suggest that the curative properties may also apply to the brain. The next step is to try to control and enhance stem cell self-healing properties with the aim of carrying out targeted therapies to a specific area of the brain.

"Our findings show that the cell capacity is much larger than we originally thought, and that these cells are very versatile," said Gesine Paul-Visse, Ph.D., Associate Professor of Neuroscience at Lund University and the study's primary author. "Most interesting is their ability to form neuronal cells, but they can also be developed for other cell types. The results contribute to better understanding of how brain cell plasticity works and opens up new opportunities to exploit these very features."

The study, published in the journal PLoS ONE, is of interest to a broad spectrum of brain research. Future possible therapeutic targets range from neurodegenerative diseases to stroke.

"We hope that our findings may lead to a new and better understanding of the brain's own repair mechanisms," said Dr. Paul-Visse. "Ultimately the goal is to strengthen these mechanisms and develop new treatments that can repair the diseased brain."

The Van Andel Institute, MSU College of Human Medicine, Saint Mary's partnership on Parkinson's research is only one example of collaboration that is lifting Medical Mile. Another is what is being done to fight cancer, the original mission of VAI.

CHAPTER NINE:
Cancer and Children on the Mile

CANCER PATIENTS HAVE NEW hope of a second chance at life because of what the researchers at Van Andel Research Institute, physicians at Spectrum Butterworth, and at least one spin-off business are discovering on the Medical Mile.

This is all happening just the way Birgit Klohs dreamed it would when she received that phone call from Dave Van Andel.

"We have enrolled some patients in clinical trials. We have actually helped some patients, kids and adults and even dogs who have cancer," said Dr. Craig Webb in his perfect British accent affected only slightly by a head cold. "So there have certainly been things that have happened well beyond our imagination."

Dr. Webb, who received his Ph.D. in cell biology from the University of East Anglia, England, in 1995, is truly one of the Medical Mile pioneers. He joined VARI as a Scientific Investigator in October 1999 and was promoted to Senior Scientific Investigator in 2008.

He is now the director of Van Andel Research Institute's Program of Translational Medicine and is proof that top talent can not only be attracted to Medical Mile, the world's best and brightest can find a home in Grand Rapids.

Dr. Webb also co-chairs the Van Andel Research Institute Pediatric Cancer Translational Research Program with nationally recognized pediatric oncologist, Dr. Giselle Sholler. She is employed by Spectrum Health Medical Group. So this is more than a theoretical partnership. This is the collaboration on Medical Mile that is saving lives by furthering cancer research.

"We are building our strengths in a focus area, which is an unmet need," Dr. Webb explained. "We (VARI) bring the science and innovation and they (Spectrum Health) bring the patients and the clinicians. I don't think either of us could do it alone."

He and Sholler are the architects of a research and discovery effort that was launched in May 2011. They began working together as the Neuroblastoma and Medulloblastoma Translational Research Consortium opened a first of its kind genomic-based clinical trial to treat and study pediatric cancer, specifically relapsed and refractory neuroblastoma.

Neuroblastoma is an especially deadly form of pediatric cancer occurring in children younger than six years old. It accounts for 15 percent of all childhood cancer deaths in the United States. Medulloblastoma is the most common malignant brain tumor. It primarily strikes children, with 71 percent of all patients diagnosed by the age of nine.

The NMTRC clinical trials are based on research from a group of closely collaborating investigators. Some of the trials are derived from a personalized medicine process and software developed at VARI. It permits near real-time processing of patient tumors and prediction of best drugs for each patient.

This is the most recent phase of a five-year process that began with proof of concept trials involving more than a dozen pediatric patients at Helen DeVos Children's Hospital in 2006.

The NMTRC, made up of 11 children's hospitals and universities offering a network of childhood cancer clinical trials, is headquartered at Van Andel Research Institute because VAI and Spectrum were able to attract Dr. Sholler to Grand Rapids.

She has conducted preclinical testing of many drugs and has conducted a Phase 1 study of the drug TPI-287 in relapsed and refractory neuroblastoma and medulloblastoma. Dr. Sholler has received funding for five years from a variety of organizations. However, a lot of the funding came from the parents of children who were suffering from cancer, people who are desperate for a breakthrough.

"This effort speaks to the sense of urgency shared by all of those involved," said VARI President and Research Director Jeffrey M. Trent Ph.D in a statement that coincided with the NMTRC announcement. "This initiative promises to have a profound impact on pediatric patients across the country and in coming years around the world."

This VARI program is intended to enable large-scale projects that will use the latest genomics and molecular analysis techniques to identify the best treatment options for children based on the individual biology of their tumor. This is a revolutionary process often referred to as "personalized medicine," something that cancer researchers on the Medical Mile have latched on to as the next wave of transformational medicine.

Webb and many other researchers on the Mile are convinced that this will be the difference between life and death for a lot of their patients. Personalized medicine means just what the phrase says. This is really groundbreaking stuff. It is so individualized or personalized that it is tailored to the patient's DNA.

Genomic-guided therapy leverages next generation sequencing and gene expression technologies to identify subtle differences in each patient. That provides doctors with a better idea of how far the cancer has progressed. It could even show doctors that a specific protein or other molecular drug target should be used for therapy.

This also involves another team effort on Medical Mile with collaboration from the Pediatric Oncology Branch at the National Cancer Institute and Grand Rapids-based Intervention Insights, a company spun out of VARI.

Webb and Sholler are only two of the players who have been brought together by the VARI-Spectrum Health partnership and the spirit of collaboration on the Mile. John Bender, Phar.D., is Clinical Operations Director, a position that is a joint appointment between VAI and Spectrum Health, which is helping to fund the Translational Orthopedic Research Program to foster long-term solutions for patients in the area of orthopedics.

Dr. Bender's background is in the assessment, development, and commercialization of therapeutics. He is playing a key role in the development of a Phase I oncology program within the newly established Center for Clinical Sciences at VAI that accelerates investigational drug and translational clinical research studies in Grand Rapids.

He also served as Director, Clinical Research - Oncology at Pfizer (Parke-Davis) for over 20 years. Early in his career, Bender worked for five years as a clinical pharmacist with the National Cancer Institute where he was heavily involved in clinical trials.

Bender most recently served as Senior Vice-President of Research and Development at Lpath, Inc., a biopharmaceutical company focused on the development and commercialization of antibodies targeted against bioactive lipids for the treatment of cancer.

He was a guest on a WOOD Radio-Clearly Community show that I hosted in September 2011 and we began by talking about a VAI event called "Help on the Hill," an excellent example of how Medical Mile is impacting healthcare in the Grand Rapids area and how it is creating a new model for the nation and perhaps the world.

"Help on the Hill" brings everyone involved in fighting cancer; doctors, researchers, patients, along with patients' friends and families together for two days on Medical Mile.

Bender told me that anyone who has ever heard the word 'cancer' and wants to know more about it was also invited to come to the Van Andel Research Institute for a Friday dinner and reception, followed by more seminars the following day, focusing on "what is brand new."

The value of openness and transparency is another lesson that is being learned on Medical Mile. This needs to be pushed forward to the next cluster formation. The community in which this new cluster is being built has to be part of the process if the people in that community are to buy into the concept.

"This is an opportunity to bring together not only researchers from Van Andel Institute, but also from all over the medical research community in Grand Rapids," Bender said, "so that the community can take advantage of the fantastic brainpower that is here."

That is a theme you will hear repeated to the point of redundancy on the Mile. The research, that will admittedly further the careers of those at the lab benches, is really not about the scientists and doctors. This work is being done for their patients, and beyond that, it is being done for the community.

The first "Help on the Hill" was so well received that it was followed by another one. "What they got out of it was a very simple layman's explanation of what cancer is, what we are doing to treat it, and since there were all the experts in the room, people had a chance to visit one-on-one with everyone in the medical community," said Bender.

This is how you build a community within a community. This event did more than give everyone involved an opportunity to find out what in the world is going on in research. It allowed patients and families to meet others who were fighting cancers, to build friendships, camaraderie, and a real community.

There is a lot to be said for feel-good events like this. But are cancer patients really getting better treatment because of what is happening on Medical Mile?

Is the Mile really that special? There are a lot of clinical operations in the U.S. Patients and their physicians are able to take advantage of cancer trials that are going on all across the country thanks to money that goes to the National Institutes of Health and in particular to the National Cancer Institute.

"However, here in West Michigan patients don't even need to leave the Grand Rapids area to avail themselves of all of those trials. There is no reason to travel to one of the big universities that surround us," Dr. Bender explained. "We have all of the medical expertise and cutting-edge clinical research that is needed right here."

Everyone on Medical Mile stresses the importance of clinical trials, and Bender concurred. He said that researchers could not make any progress unless they had those trials to answer the questions "is this new therapy useful, does it work, how safe is it and how does it compare to what is already have available to us?"

That is why Medical Mile needs patients from across the nation and around the world to come to Grand Rapids. That is why the effort to convince doctors to send their patients to the Mile instead of the Mayo or Cleveland clinics is so important.

The process of creating a new drug is incredibly expensive and time consuming. It will be 10 years before the drugs that are being developed on the Mile ever get close to a patient in a clinical trial. The complete development process for a new compound takes 13 years.

So by the time they get to a patient the research team has a pretty good idea of what a drug is going to do, what they are going to see, what dosage is needed, and then they verify that in clinical trials.

Yet, failure is always an option, according to Bender.

"If we do our best effort, and it does not work, we go back and look at something else."

A new drug or treatment is not the first option for a patient in a clinical trial. "If you have a new diagnosis, no one is going to come up to you and say, 'why don't we forget standard therapy. Let's try this new drug,'" said Bender. That is not going to happen. It is simply not an ethical thing to do.

However, many of the therapies fail right out of the gate, or they don't work nearly as well as the medical team would like them too. And often the new drugs stop working after a short period of time. So the question becomes 'what now?'"

"Grand Rapids has a very, very unusual concentration of medical expertise (on Medical Mile) that you find very rarely throughout the United States," Dr. Bender explained. "People in Grand Rapids probably don't realize how special this area is in terms of medical competency and medical research."

"Some of the people I work with are definitely some of the best and brightest in the world of medicine."

The interaction of the Medical Mile institutions, these entities that are competitive by nature, is unusual. Most major universities want to do everything themselves. The world of science and research is incredibly competitive. Silo-mentality and the refusal to share for fear of losing an advantage is the norm. However, that is not the way it is on Medical Mile, according to Dr. Bender.

"We all realize that none of us are as smart as all of us," he explained, "so we all collaborate and use what we each bring to the table in the most efficient process."

Craig Webb had been working, really living, on the Mile for a little more than 12 years when we met in the VARI lobby. The first five of those years were spent working across the street in the Oncology Department at Spectrum.'

The pioneers on Medical Mile, like Webb, were right in the middle of its creation. "We used to put our hard hats on and come across on a daily basis to see what was going on here," said Webb. "We would get our lunch at the Burger King across the street that was torn down to make way for the cancer pavilion."

Dr. Webb has also seen internal changes. VAI has gone through cycles of programmatical developments. When new partners are brought in, it changes the dynamics a little bit politically. Adjustments have to be made. They have done that.

He described the VARI on southwest end of Medical Mile, wrapped around a 19th century church, Immanuel Lutheran (the typo that the editor couldn't find), as "second to none." They had 250 people on the payroll when Webb and I spoke.

"We have capacity for 800 people so we have to hire. Attracting talent to West Michigan is challenging sometimes when we are competing with the likes of the East and West coasts. So, I think we are going to have to be a bit more creative around the way we do that here."

But it is getting easier. Selling Grand Rapids used to be his first challenge when Webb went on the road to talk about the work being done at Van Andel Research Institute and on Medical Mile.

"Today, I don't have to spend so much time explaining what Grand

Rapids is, and we have published many papers so we are known as an institution, at least," he said. "My experience has been that if we can get them to come the first time and take a look at the place, we can get them to stay."

Of course acceptance goes both ways. This is where the new openness and transparency model comes into play. The Grand Rapids community really didn't know what was going on inside Van Andel Research Institute nor did it really grasp the concept of what was possible along Medical Mile when VARI opened its doors.

Something like this just was not in the Grand Rapids DNA. We had been the home of industrialists, not Nobel Prize winners. We had been the home of people who made chairs, desks, tables, and automotive parts, not people who were trying to cure cancer. And we really were not sure just what was happening inside that odd-shaped building, filled not with blue collars and wrenches, but white lab coats and Petri dishes.

"We have become more transparent in what we do. That has helped and I think the community has become genuinely proud of what Medical Mile has accomplished," he said. "They have always been very warm and receptive of what was happening here."

Dr. Bender believes Medical Mile has impacted Grand Rapids. "It has been a landmark change for the Grand Rapids area. When I got here about a year and a half ago there were building cranes all over and I thought, 'don't these people know there is a recession going on?"

Bender also maintained progress is being made in the war on cancer and said that beyond the partnerships and the success on Medical Mile what has changed dramatically has come about because of what taxpayers have contributed to the National Institutes of Health for the human genome program.

This is another important lesson that the Medical Mile offers. The partnerships that are making it work include a real public-private model that involves state and federal governments.

Bender told me that the effort to investigate personalized cancer treatment based on each patient's DNA would not have come as far as it has without researchers finding out more about the human genome. And that would not have happened without National Institutes of Health funding.

"It cost us $3 billion to do that work. Was it worth it? Absolutely, much, much more than you will ever know. It allows us to do is to take a piece of tissue from a patient and use that information to decide what disease they have and pick drugs for the patient."

Webb believes Medical Mile has the potential to become a global player in the health and life sciences arena. But that had not happened yet, as we spoke. "You have to become recognized for something first before you get invited into the club of the global community," said Webb. "We have done some of that. We have become established and are known for certain areas of research like personalized medicine."

To take the Mile to that next level, Webb sees the need for a change in the organizational structure of the Medical Mile. He believes the emphasis should be, along with attracting top-level talent, continuing to put together the connectivity between programs and institutions that will allow the Mile to reach its potential.

Going forward, Dr. Webb would like to see a more unified effort on the Mile. "You can't be everything for everyone," he stressed. "We have to decide now where we want to be particularly strong, what areas, what programs, and where we would be happy to place the "B" team. We can't be the "A" team in all of those things."

The big challenge for Medical Mile is one of organization as Dr. Webb sees it, with each institution facing its own set of initiatives, challenges and goals. However, he also sees a need for a Medical Mile-wide umbrella organization.

"To form good programs we need a blend of administrative oversight with functional leadership," he said. "Putting together some SWAT teams across partners in these areas of emphasis, teams that go across institutional lines will be important. I don't think any of these institutions will be able to do it all by themselves."

Medical Mile is a balancing act. The Grand Rapids medical community's C-suite executive leadership does not meet in a formal, regular fashion. They do speak to each other, but the players maintain their individual identities and missions. There is no "Medical Mile Czar." There doesn't have to be. It is that shared vision, the collective insight, the belief that they are much stronger together than they could ever be separately and the inter-dependency of a cluster of prosperity that guides the Mile.

There are some weeks that it works better than others. Just ask the man who drives the biggest institution on the Mile, Spectrum Health Systems, Inc.

CHAPTER TEN:
The Marriage

THE DAY WHEN GRAND Rapids really sat up and took notice of Medical Mile was the day that we learned Rahn Bentley had a new heart beating in his chest thanks to surgeons at Meijer Heart Center, part of Spectrum Health Systems, Inc.

"It really helps getting through the grieving process," Peggy Korzen said of donating her husband Tim's heart. "The next best thing is seeing that his heart lives on through somebody else." [13]

Tim Korzen's heart is beating in the chest of 51-year old Rahn Bentley, the first of 11 people to receive a heart transplant at Spectrum Health's Meijer Heart Center on the Medical Mile. Bentley received his new heart, in November 2010. He is a survivor to be celebrated.

The Korzen-Bentley heart transplant came as a total surprise to the Grand Rapids community. It really turned our attitudes inside out to think that we could do this. Heart transplants could be performed in West Michigan.

We were amazed. But think about how this must have rocked the world of Rahn Bentley and his twin brother Ray, a former linebacker for the Buffalo Bills, whom you may have seen on Fox TV NFL broadcasts and who was heard on WOOD-AM radio for several years in Grand Rapids.

Ray said that he and Rahn were told two days after Thanksgiving Day

---

13   Corey Morse, "Rahn Bentley Talks About Heart Transplant" *M-Live. com, The Grand Rapids Press*, Nov. 5, 2011. Accessed May 26, 2012.

http://photos.mlive.com/grandrapidspress/2011/11/rahn_bentley_talks_about_heart_4.html

2010 that a heart had been found, and the operation had to happen in a few hours.

"I've played in Super Bowls, and it doesn't even come close to seeing my brother when he woke up," said Ray. "We were both crying and holding each other. Our birthday was Thanksgiving, so this was a hell of a present."[14]

Nine of the other 11 transplant patients from that first year are doing well. The tenth died after contracting an infection following the surgery.

The heart transplant and heart surgical teams that performed the Korzen-Bentley transplant make up the Richard DeVos Heart and Lung Transplant Program that along with a heart failure program is part of the Frederick Meijer Heart & Vascular Institute.

Anyone in the Midwest and certainly everyone in Grand Rapids will recognize the Meijer name. For the uninitiated, the Meijer family is responsible for Meijer Inc., the retail chain whose superstores are said, in West Michigan at least, to have inspired Sam Walton.

This is another case of a family with money, giving money. It is also another case study that shows us there are no silos on Medical Mile.

The Meijer Institute's emphasis on research includes partnering with Van Andel Institute and Michigan State University College of Human Medicine. A Spectrum statement issued in July 2010 said the Institute's efforts would "focus on translational research that begins in the lab and progresses to clinical trials for people with diseases such as heart failure, acute coronary syndromes and heart arrhythmias.

What does that really mean for Spectrum Health, Medical Mile and the Grand Rapids community? Spectrum Health System EVP and Hospital Group President Matt Van Vranken put it best when he also said, "we view the formation of the Frederik Meijer Heart and Vascular Institute as the beginning of the transformation for Spectrum Health that takes us from a regional leader to national leadership in heart care."

If that happens, you know the "trickle down" will only add to the reinvention of this American community.

The Butterworth Hospital-Blodgett Memorial Medical Center merger

---

14   Kayla King, "How Rahn Bentley came to be Grand Rapids first heart transplant patient on Saturday" *M-Live.com The Grand Rapids Press* Nov. 30, 2010. Accessed May 26, 2012. http://www.mlive.com/news/grand-rapids/index. ssf/2010/11/how_rahn_bentley_came_to_be_gr.html

that created Spectrum Health Systems was as important to the creation of the Medical Mile as was the billion dollar check written by Jay Van Andel that launched Van Andel Institute.

This marriage was not a Romeo and Juliet story. These parents wanted it to happen. But still it was very contentious. The Federal Trade Commission tried to block the merger arguing that it would kill health care competition in metro Grand Rapids. Nobody disputed it would create a medical industry titan. Paperwork filed for the merger predicted that Spectrum Health would control "somewhere between 47 and 65 percent of the market for general acute care inpatient hospital services" and as much as "70 percent of the primary care inpatient hospital market." [15]

A district court ruling and the appeal to the U.S. Sixth Circuit Court of Appeals went against the FTC. Promises of $6 million going to serve the health care needs of the poor and $170 million in capital and operating cost savings outweighed the monopoly argument. In addition to accepting those promises that were made in writing, the Sixth Circuit Court judges couldn't see how the Spectrum Board of Trustees would have any interest in raising prices "above competitive levels."

The Blodgett and Butterworth boards promised a three-year price freeze on hospital charges, followed by a four-year limit to hospital price increases.

Spectrum's board would include eight representatives from Blodgett, eight from Butterworth and another eight who had not served on either board. This would equal unprecedented community involvement in health care.

The Hillman Commission, in 1994, recommended the hospitals, physicians or both consolidate services. At the time, Blodgett Medical Center was a 410-bed, acute care regional teaching hospital in Grand Rapids. Blodgett was known for its emphasis in heart and vascular, emergency/trauma, women and family, digestive diseases, cancer treatment and more than 30 specialty clinics at 15 community hospitals.

Butterworth, at the time of the merger, was a 529-bed acute care regional teaching hospital that was linked to more than a dozen community hospitals in West Michigan, along with primary care centers.

Was it a marriage of equals? Not really. Is any marriage that? Was yours? This wasn't either. Butterworth was regional. Butterworth had its flag planted a century ago on the southern shoulders of Michigan Street

---

15   No. 96-2440 U.S. Court of Appeals for the Sixth Circuit, Plaintiff-Appellant v. Butterworth Health Corporation and Blodgett Medical Center

NE, the future home of the Medical Mile. And Butterworth had Rich DeVos.

The man who made Amway, and in partnership with the other large money in town, made Grand Rapids what it was in the latter decades of the 20th century, was the chairman of the Butterworth board when all of this was happening. Remember, behind the scenes the top players in town were already talking about the concept of a medical campus on Michigan Street NE. Butterworth was already buying up property on what would be the hottest mile in Grand Rapids.

The sheriff that performed this ceremony, the Sixth Circuit Court gave its blessing to the union in a 1997 ruling that supported District Judge David McKeague, when he refused an FTC bid to stop the marriage. That nod was as good as a ring. Without a shotgun, Rich DeVos at Butterworth and David Wagner, chairman of the Blodgett Board of Trustees had everything they needed. Their children were married.

That is not to say that this has been a happy marriage from day-one, or that the jilted have no hard feelings. Again, this is real life. When the honeymoon ends, the imperfections become apparent.

But all hard feelings aside, from our 2012 perspective, the merger did not kill competition. Saint Mary's Health and Metro Health are alive and well, both serving as parts of the Medical Mile community albeit it geographically removed from the shoulders of Michigan Street NE.

They have also been able to carry on with their lives, forming their own medical communities that will be explored in the coming chapters.

The consummation of the Butterworth-Blodgett marriage created the largest not-for-profit health care system in West Michigan. Spectrum is the umbrella for nine hospitals, 190 service sites and 1,938 beds statewide. That includes Helen DeVos Children's Hospital, a big, beautiful, blue building on the Medical Mile, the Meijer Heart Center just down the Mile to the east, and the Lemmen Holton Cancer Pavilion across the street on the northern shoulders of Michigan Street, built on land that was occupied by a Burger King restaurant.

The opening of Helen DeVos Children's Hospital was another "look at what we have done" moment on Medical Mile. This newest hospital in Grand Rapids was built adjacent to Spectrum-Butterworth Hospital. It changed the Medical Mile's skyline on the southern shoulders of Michigan Street NE.

When someone says "you can't miss it," they are telling the truth. It is the tallest, roundest, bluest building on the Mile with a glass-covered blue bridge that matches the hospital and arches over the spine of Michigan Street NE, carrying children and their parents from shoulder to shoulder of this Atlas of healthcare in West Michigan.

It includes an outdoor garden and private inpatient rooms that are large enough to allow parents to stay overnight with their children, and there is room for the family to play. This really is all about the children.

When Rich and Helen DeVos wrote the check that made this institution possible, Rich also said that if you are going to build a hospital for children, it has to have a place where parents can buy ice cream for the patients. So, it does.

And what kid doesn't like pizza? Spectrum hired a chef from one of Grand Rapids' best Italian restaurants to take care of that

That is not to downplay the quality of care at DeVos Children's Hospital, however this anecdote had to be included to demonstrate the "children first" attitude inside this facility that is making the Medical Mile a magnet for pediatric care in Michigan.

DeVos Children's Hospital is changing the way our children are cared for. It is also saving the lives of what we care for most, our children, like little Levi Schoenborn.

Melissa and Martin Schoenborn's baby boy had never been sick a day in his toddling life until he got close to his first birthday. It happened very quickly. Ten-month old Levi had trouble breathing in March 2009. Melissa and Martin rushed him to DeVos Children's Hospital where he was placed on a ventilator in the 24-bed pediatric critical care unit. The problem, as noted in a Spectrum Health Systems media release, was respiratory syncytial, an infection of the lungs and breathing passages.

A respiratory therapist "talked softly and stroked Levi's hair to soothe the restless boy in the middle of the night," according to Spectrum literature that told the story, and "a nurse encouraged Melissa to help bathe Levi to reinforce the mother and child bond."

It worked. Levi is alive and well. He is a "busy 2-year old" in the words of his mom, more than a year after his hospitalization.

Makenzie Hollister was admitted to the hospital before Levi got there. She was one of the first patients to walk through the doors of this big blue building to see the children-inspired and drawn art decorating the walls when it opened Jan. 11, 2012. Makenzie, as noted in a Spectrum Health Services media release, was in the hospital again, exactly one year later, as hospital administrators, staff, patients and the Grand Rapids community marked the anniversary of this building that is changing the way we are caring for our kids in West Michigan.

She and her twin sister Shelbie, who were both born premature, are regulars. They still see multiple specialists at Children's Hospital including those who specialize in nephrology, pulmonary, ophthalmology, cardiology and endocrinology.

The Hollister girls were two of more than 8,300 children admitted to DeVos Children's Hospital in its new building on Medical Mile, as *Last Chance Mile* was being written. More than 6,600 surgeries were performed in the building, there were better than 41,300 emergency room visits, more than 53,000 radiology procedures and more than 28,000 pizzas and 5,700 gallons of ice cream sold and served in the hospital's Balke Café.

Danielle Swett is another "survivor" whose story is told by Spectrum Health and celebrated at DeVos Children's Hospital. The little girl, adopted from China by Paul and Paula Swett, had an opening between two major blood vessels in her heart. Danielle was the first patient treated in the new hospital's pediatric heart catheterization laboratory.

Through two needle-sized opening in Danielle's leg, Dr. Ronald Grifka, division chief of pediatric cardiology, repaired the hole in her heart by inserting a special plug. Danielle went home that night and was back in school a few days later.

Richard Breon keeps it all running as the president and CEO of Spectrum. He is also one of the players who put the Medical Mile together and remembers it as not quite serendipitous, but not really happening on purpose.

"We had plans of developing buildings around certain clinic services like heart, children's and cancer," Breon told me. "The parts and pieces were out there, but I don't think they were joined together very well at the time."

The collaboration that made the Medical Mile could be called an evolutionary process, according to Breon. The Medical Mile neighbors had fences. They have yet to take them down. However they slowly began talking over those fences. It was not always smooth. It never is. And it still is not. These are all individual players with their own goals, their own egos. There is no Medical Mile Czar running this.

"It came with its starts and stops. I think there were times when there was a lot of good conversation around the table and there were times when there wasn't as much. I think that was to be expected," said Breon. "Everyone kind of had their own ideas."

However, the discussions of the Medical Mile's future hit an "ah-ha" moment when the players saw they did have all of the pieces and parts they needed to form this new cluster of prosperity. It must have been like dumping a jig saw puzzle out of the box, turning all of the pieces over, and realizing you have everything you need. You just have to put it all together.

"We saw that this really could be something. This could be significant for this community," said Breon. "As this thing grew, and the conversation developed, I think we saw that."

Of all the people I spoke with about the Medical Mile, Breon was the first to say that the concept of this cluster of prosperity was oversold in the beginning. Now, he feels better about it, telling me we are in a time of "realistic expectation."

"In the beginning there was an over-abundance of enthusiasm that never could have been met," he explained. "People were thinking of all of these trickle-down economic benefits from all of these life sciences companies that were going to be moving in here and billions of dollars in revenue that would be generated."

It was a bit overwhelming.

Breon thinks Grand Rapids now understands that it takes generations to bulldoze, dig, shovel and build that kind of business landscape change. However, it is starting to happen. Grand Rapids is farther ahead that it was a dozen years ago when Breon first sat down in his executive office.

To begin with, it is much easier for the Mile to attract real talent.

To demonstrate that, he told a short story of the quest to attract a high-level neurosurgeon, someone with a strong desire for clinical care, but who also wanted to do bench research. This echoes what Rich Cook told me at WMSTI and it is the model that Birgit Klohs foresaw when she picked up the phone and heard Dave Van Andel's voice telling her our world was about to change.

"You can attract a person like that here because you have a research institute (Van Andel Institute) right next door," said Breon. "You have strong clinical care right next door, and that person would always want a medical school affiliation. And now we have that available."

The community has been built. This is like the subdivisions that sprang up after World War Two. Once the lawns were seeded, all the schools were built, shopping centers with acres of free parking constructed, all they needed was Baby Boomers in diapers. Thanks to ex-GIs, their wives and pent-up hormones that wasn't a problem.

The pieces and parts have been put together on the Medical Mile. The institutions are in place and operating as smoothly as a BMW sliding through what we call the S-Curve on U.S. 131 in the heart of downtown Grand Rapids.

More importantly, attitudes are evolving. Breon agreed that the Grand Rapids community's self-image has changed. There has also been a transformation in the way the medical, life sciences and bio-tech worlds outside of West Michigan see Grand Rapids.

Still though, it all comes down to those people of different religions, creeds, colors and nationalities, who are running across the spine of Michigan Street NE 24-7, 52 weeks a year, sweating in the summer, shivering in the winter, sneezing in the spring and doing whatever they do in the autumn.

"It isn't just the facilities. It is the substance behind the facilities," he said. "It is also the commitment that they see here and the depth of the services that are provided here. That is really what the Medical Mile is."

There is an "ah-ha" moment. It shows the unanimity of feeling that while the Mile may be the star, the street and its buildings are not the real story. The people inside those buildings are the story.

As has been cited before in this book —and this is a great lesson to remember for the creation of the next cluster of prosperity—talent attracts talent and talent talks to talent. Breon point out that the people who are working on the Mile are the best recruiters Grand Rapids has. "These people are talking to their peers around the world," Breon pointed out. "They will be the ones at conferences who are talking it up. We like to have people at the podium, not just in the audience."

Breon agreed that it is also important to convince "that doctor in Tupelo" as Alliance for Health President Lody Zwarensteyn put it, to refer his patients to the Medical Mile. But Breon doesn't think we should put too much emphasis on that. He comes close to paraphrasing that old political cliché when he said that essentially most health care is local, or at least it is rendered close by.

"The Mayo Clinic, for instance, gets most of its patients from inside a 90-mile radius around Rochester, Minnesota," he said.

The Medical Mile and Spectrum Health should be doing whatever can be done to attract patients from outside West Michigan. They are needed for clinical trials. Their new money is certainly welcomed. It is happening. But again, Breon believes it is important to manage expectations.

"This is not something that magically happens with the flip of a switch," he stressed. "It is a process of building it, building on it, building it and building on it. It isn't one day you have none and the next day you have everyone in the world coming in."

That could be one of the best lessons learned in the conference room with Rick Breon for that next cluster of prosperity. Expectations have to be controlled. The next cluster should not be oversold. "Patience is a virtue," said Breon.

So, what does he believe is a "realistic expectation" for the Medical Mile?

"You could see some cutting edge research. You could see some translational research, what you do at the bench being put to some good use with patients," he forecast. "I don't know if you will see 'cures' for things, but you could. That is certainly a possibility. "

Most importantly, Breon can see Grand Rapids becoming a destination for health care. Even though that is a phrase and a goal that was probably overused in the creation of the Medical Mile, he can see the day when people who have never been close to Grand Rapids come to the city for health care.

Heart transplants –the Meijer Heart Center was up to 17 of those operations as this book was being published—are critical, in fact. But Breon pointed out there are also a lot of "bread and butter" services that the Mile has to perform first.

"You have to deliver babies well," he said. "It isn't all the high esoteric things. Those numbers just aren't big enough."

Spectrum also does its share of clinical, translational research. Breon thinks the organization needs that as well as patient care, but there is no doubt which he feels is more important.

"We like to describe our model as a tricycle," he explained. "The big wheel in the front is patient care. The two smaller wheels in the back are medical education and research. It doesn't mean they are not important. It means they are not as important."

It's kind of a medical trinity for Spectrum, as Breon sees it, "We do education. We do research. We take care of people."

By keeping those agendas in synch, each adds value to the other.

So, the institutions joined together by the marriage that made Spectrum and the neighborhood that is the Medical Mile are doing well. What about the broken hearted? Where do they go? They rebound and build their own lives and their own communities.

CHAPTER ELEVEN:
Independent and Proud

Metro Health has always been different, independent and proud of it. That has never been easy and it certainly was more than just "not easy" when it was time for Metro to move out of the southeast side Grand Rapids neighborhood that had been its home for 50 years. Everyone wanted this health care group to be part of the Medical Mile, except Metro Health.

Metro Health is the youngest health care organization in Grand Rapids by at least a century. It came into existence as Grand Rapids Osteopathic Hospital one year after Pearl Harbor was attacked.

Grand Rapids' men were at war. The city's women were at work. Still, a group of osteopathic doctors were able to raise just over $24,000 in pledges, enough to open their first hospital inside a three-story, English-style mansion on Lake Drive in an affluent southeast side Grand Rapids neighborhood. It had been the home of the Most Rev. Joseph C. Plagens, Bishop of the Diocese of Grand Rapids. Now it was home to the first osteopathic hospital in Grand Rapids, run by the people who would eventually build Metropolitan Hospital, a two-story facility with elevators.

That was the technology the founding physicians were missing. They launched their hospital with three-floors of medical care, but not a single elevator. Ever carry a pregnant woman, in labor, up three flights of stairs? They did it at Grand Rapids Osteopathic Hospital because there was no other choice. "(However) the staff never tripped nor dropped a patient," said Dr. Richard Bethune, son of a GROH founding physician.

While they were in the Most Rev. Plagens' former residence they did what they had to do. If an oxygen tank on the first floor was needed on the third floor, it was put on someone's shoulder and carried. People who worked there had to be smart, committed and strong, or at the very least, physically fit.

While hammers and saws were still being used to finish the renovation, physicians' wives were holding sewing bees, stitching supplies, making bandages, doing the cooking in their homes and bringing meals to patients. The wives who held nursing degrees worked alongside their husbands.

A couple of years later, the doctors bought the house next door, expanding their hospital into that building.

It still wasn't big enough, so another group of Grand Rapids osteopaths opened Burton Heights Osteopathic Hospital in an old funeral home. Eventually, the founders of GROH raised enough money to build a two-story hospital on a 12-acre parcel on the southeast side of Grand Rapids. It was in basically the same neighborhood as Rev. Plagens' former home, less than four miles away from the section of Michigan Street NE that would become, in another half-century, the Medical Mile.

In 1959, the two groups merged their facilities, expanding Grand Rapids Osteopathic to 138 beds.

That still wasn't large enough. GROH remodeled once to increase capacity in 1962, then a couple of years later, launched a $2 million expansion that was completed in time for the GROH 25th anniversary in 1967.[16]

However, there was still a problem. They were landlocked. GROH just could not grow anymore, surrounded by the neighborhood that existed before the hospital landed in the middle of it. Something had to be done.

This turned into a real political donnybrook played out on the front pages of The Grand Rapids Press, in the 1990's. For the most part, Grand Rapids kept its dirty laundry behind closed doors. This time, we were invited into the laundromat.

Metropolitan Hospital's neighbors – it had been renamed by the time the battle broke – didn't want it to go. It is not that they loved Metro and all the noise, traffic and people that go with a hospital, it is just that sometimes the devil you know....well, you know.

Metro has always been the underdog in Grand Rapids' health care community. Board Chair Doyle Hayes is that way, too. He is a middle-aged man who made his money in the auto supply business, but never the kind of cash that a DeVos or a Van Andel could lay claim to. And one more thing,

---

16   Michael Lozon with John Leegwater, *Transplanting the Passion, Metro Health's Journey from Neighborhood Hospital to Health-Care Village*, (Wyoming: Metro Health Hospital 2007), 1-11

Doyle Hayes is an African-American in a city whose power structure was as white as white could be.

Of course he was right in the middle of this fight. Hayes was at, what he told me was, "an angry neighborhood group," meeting at a Presbyterian Church discussing Metro's future. Metro's board really wanted to stay. They had purchased several homes in the neighborhood, but couldn't get everything they needed to expand the way they felt the hospital need to grow.

Metro had offered people one-and-a-half times the value of their homes, "but at some point we realized we just couldn't buy up enough homes to expand," Hayes remembered. "That neighborhood deserved better."

They searched several other neighborhoods in the city. Hayes really felt they had exhausted all of their options. So the conversation turned at that neighborhood meeting when he said. "I think we are going to have to move."

"And you could hear a pin drop when I said that," Hayes told me. "Apparently some of the neighbors didn't want us to move. Someone asked what would happen if we moved. I was kind of pissed so I said, 'I don't know. Could be a minimum security prison or it could be anthrax production, I don't know. Well, Mike (Faas, Metro Health President and CEO) said, 'Doyle you can't talk to these people anymore.'"

From that point on, Metro started making plans to move.

With that settled, wouldn't it make sense to move Metro to Michigan Street, or at least to downtown Grand Rapids as part of the vision of making the area a medical destination? Why wouldn't it be in Metro's best interest to do that? Downtown Grand Rapids was filled with empty buildings, not on the scale of what you see in Detroit today, but still, there was plenty of space for, shall we call it, urban renewal?

The idea of moving Metro downtown made sense to everyone except the people at Metro. They were like Kevin in the movie, "Home Alone." Everyone was on board except him. And, he was the only one who knew it.

Metro built its own health care community, in a cornfield.

"Their rational was really kind of shallow," said Alliance for Health (AFH) President Lodewyk (Lody) Zwarensteyn. "They said, 'we have to have a suburban hospital,' and I said, 'Sure, but which direction, north, south, east or west.' Maybe we need four suburban hospitals. Why don't we put one in Rockford? I mean, come on.' I was very vocal."

Lody, and the Special Kent County Area Health Care Facilities Study, organized by AFH and chaired by U.S. District Judge Douglas Hillman didn't see any sense in establishing a "suburban hospital."

The Hillman Commission decided, "If we put things together we get a synergy where the whole is greater than the sum of the parts. And that is what we are getting downtown (Grand Rapids)," Zwarensteyn said. "But (now) for most people outside of the community, Metro (Hospital) becomes an afterthought. You don't think of them as being part of this core."

Metro Health CEO Michael Faas would beg to disagree. He does not view Medical Mile as a straight line and certainly not a single street on the north side of Grand Rapids. This is yet another lesson to take into the future. Grand Rapids is more than just Grand Rapids. It really has to be because the future belongs to "mega cities" or "mega communities" that can offer lifestyles and opportunities that just are not available in small towns.

And one more lesson: never underestimate an organization that is determined to be independent. Metro's board of trustees didn't just move a hospital. They built a community. Yet, it is still part of Medical Mile.

Faas pointed out during our conversation in his Health Village office that Metro has a surgery center on the Medical Mile and besides that, he believes the Mile is a virtual, not literal, concept.

Spectrum Health CEO Rick Breon told us that most medical service is local. Faas also pointed out that hospitals and providers concentrate on serving a primary service area within a 120-mile-radius. So it follows that, "Every health care provider in this community is really part of Medical Mile," Faas said. "Metro is a building block of Medical Mile."

"We are all attached to it by a set of strings. Some of those strings are as wide as streets and some are threadbare. There are a lot of attachments and all together it is a pretty strong rope that holds us."

He also said the attachment of Metro as "part and parcel" of Medical Mile is proven by Metro's medical staff. While they are independent, Faas believes they are "dead loyal" to Metro even though they interact with everything that is going on, on the Medical Mile.

"At the upper level, we always get along. At the upper level we always support each other. That I think is why we are all part of Medical Mile," said Faas. "It is not always open cooperation. But it is understanding and acceptance. That is right on the edge of collaboration."

Collaboration should not be confused with consolidation. Faas is a big believer in independence. "What we feel is in the best interest of everyone is choice and balance," he said. "No organization can take care of everything, and one size does not fit all."

Faas and Metro have not been limited by a lack of imagination or ambition. This underdog organization in the West Michigan healthcare community not only decided not to build on the Medical Mile, they moved as far away as possible and they created a totally new concept called Health Village.

Metro's 170-acre Health Village is as revolutionary in its way as Medical Mile. Metro grew its own community in a cornfield, a community that would uplift the city of Wyoming and southern Kent County as much as the Medical Mile has revitalized Grand Rapids. Just like Medical Mile is more than any one of the institutions on Michigan Street NE, Health Village is much more than just Metro Hospital.

It includes a Hyatt Place Hotel for families and friends who need a place to stay while loved ones are hospitalized. Of course it has the medical offices and other health related businesses that you would expect to be built near a hospital. Health Village also includes Sarah Care Adult Day Services, The Cancer Center at Metro Health Village and Frog Hollow, the City of Wyoming's fully accessible playground for children, and the Spartan Stores YMCA.

Faas said every entity is a partner with Metro and Metro is a partner with each of them. Each one makes the other stronger, creating a magnet for patient health care. The hospital is really like an anchor store in a mall, or a courthouse in a small town square. It is the nucleus that everything else spins around.

"We just hit our 1000th tour, if that tells you anything," said Faas. "People have come from 30 countries and four continents to see what we have done. It (Health Village) has been copied in Nebraska, in Colorado, California, and we have heard that somebody in Arizona is copying in the concept."

This all came from a cornfield.

Dr. William "Bill" Cunningham was Metro's Chief Medical Officer when this concept was created and walked the field before the first spade of earth was turned.

"We got muddy," he chuckled, recalling what it was like to walk through the cornfields, trying to visualize what this acreage would look like with a hospital sitting on the property.

"It was a lot of fun," Cunningham also remembered. "The biggest thing about planning for this was that before we put a shovel in the ground the administration, the doctors and the people in this community were all in sync, and said this is what they wanted too."

Cunningham, Mike Faas, John Leegwater and board chair Doyle Hayes went across the United States looking for a model on which they could build Health Village.

"But there weren't any," said Cunningham. "It (Health Village) was fashioned from what we saw down in Naples, Florida, over in Oregon and in Connecticut."

Cunningham and the others set up what they called the "War Room" where they pasted everything that they thought should be part of the vision for this new health care community up on the walls.

"Mike (Faas) looked at it, and said, 'you've got something here, let's run with it and make this a community," he recalled.

Cunningham told me that Metro's board and administration were true believers in the concept of a suburban hospital. "Remember these discussions started around the time of 9-11," he said. "And we thought that if there was, let's say, a bio-terrorism attack downtown, it would be important to have a hospital out here."

True enough. But it also made sense for a hospital that has always valued its own identity, its independence and having its own way of doing things.

"Another part of our vision was that with a suburban hospital, you didn't have to go down to Medical Mile," said Cunningham. It is easy to understand why Spectrum and other players on the Mile would have a problem with that.

It was a bold stroke that also came at the same time as a new expressway, M-6, was built in southern Kent County opening a new population center that is in the shape of a pie wedge, growing faster than any other wedge in Michigan.

When Metro announced plans to open Health Village, coupled with the news that M-6 would be built in southern Kent County, Wyoming city officials rejoiced, hoping it would replace blue collars with white lab coats just as the Medical Mile was doing in Grand Rapids.

And it has. In a way, Health Village has been more of a turnaround catalyst than Medical Mile. Cornfields have become retail and business centers. Southern Kent County has become suburbanized thanks to Metro's vision.

There is no doubt that Health Village has changed the culture of southern Kent County.

This took courage. There were naysayers in the beginning and plenty of pressure to stay in Grand Rapids. Faas admits they had to change some minds to make this work.

"I called it 'Transplanting the Passion,' and a big part of that was keeping the doctors and staff who were with us, with us, and not having them decide they didn't want to drive out to our new site," he recalled. "It worked. We kept 95 percent of both the employee and physician bases."

That plays right into Faas' overriding philosophy that a hospital is not just a brick-and-mortar building. A hospital is the people who take care of the patients, one patient at a time. Beyond all of the technology, and the amenities, it all comes down to that one person or the several people who touch the patient.

"That is what I was most worried about," explained Faas. "Could we take the good stuff? There was a lot of stuff I was willing to leave on Boston Street and have it demolished with our old building. But gladly we were able to take the good stuff with us."

Part of that "good stuff" was, and is, Michigan State University.

Metro has its own relationship with Michigan State University that is totally separate from what is happening on the geographical—as opposed to virtual-- Medical Mile. This Metro-MSU bond has been in place for far longer than the MSU College of Human Medicine has had a Michigan Street NE mailing address.

The Michigan State University College of Osteopathic Medicine campus is a part of Metro Health. Close to 100 students, interns and residents in Osteopathy Medicine are at Metro, and about half of those come from Michigan State. MSU Spartans, yes, but they are not part of the College of Human Medicine located on Michigan Street NE.

This is where the lesson of never underestimating an organization with a dream to remain free and independent is really driven home. Here is also where it becomes evident that the simmering tension between Metro and Spectrum has not gone away.

"One of the most exciting things we are working on is crafting choice so that a virtual monopoly (Spectrum Health) does not become a real one," said Faas, "so the Medical Mile is really a West Michigan venture not limited by a five-block street."

They might not have liked it, but Spectrum Health and Saint Mary's Health Care set up shop as close to Metro Health Village as they could, as quickly as possible. Actually, they got there first.

"Imitation is the sincerest form of flattery, and that is exactly what happened," said Cunningham, pointing out that Saint Mary's and Spectrum opened their suburban locations before Metro Hospital was ready to go.

"And guess what?" Cunningham said. "The suburbs just got healthier because the people here no longer had to go all the way downtown for their health care."

Faas believes healthcare is moving to what he sees as "integration."

"There are two ways that can happen. One is consolidation: ownership, command and control," he said. "And there are those who, without naming names, are already doing that."

Faas is convinced that independent collaboration as compared to collaboration by acquisition is the path that would be best for the West Michigan community, the patients, health care providers and of course, Medical Mile, be it virtual or literal.

"We believe that by a series of joint ventures, partnerships and relationships, we can build something that goes to the same end point, collaboration, and at the same time actually craft choice in the marketplace."

Let's put a name on this. He was talking about Pennant Health Alliance. Basically it is an organization of health care providers in West Michigan, without Spectrum Health. Faas also serves as its CEO.

Pennant Health Alliance, at the time of this writing, involved Metro Health and Trinity Health, which includes another player on Medical Mile, Saint Mary's Health Care along with hospitals in Battle Creek, Muskegon, Cadillac and Grayling, Mich., and the University of Michigan Health System.

This alliance has size: Nine hospitals, 110-plus outpatient and medical office settings, a service area that covers 3.8 million people in 43 counties, more than 3,200 physicians, 30,525 associates, and total revenue of $3.6 billion.

"Metro's role in this (Pennant) is to prove that an independent hospital can exist and stay independent, be a choice in the market , but still take advantage of all the things that we are not right now, like size and scale," explained Faas.

Metro is not the only voice of independence in the Grand Rapids health care community. Nor is it the only health care entity that has created its own community. Saint Mary's has done that, too.

CHAPTER TWELVE:
A Mini-Mile

THE INSTITUTION PHIL McCORKLE runs may not be on Michigan Street, but Saint Mary's Health Care is still a key part of the Medical Mile healthcare-life sciences cluster. It is part of the support system that keeps Michigan Street NE alive, and always awake.

As Birgit Klohs would point out more than 15 years after the first ground on Michigan Street was broken for the Mile, "this (Medical Mile) is not a straight line."

Healthcare in Grand Rapids without Saint Mary's would be unimaginable. It has always been at the urban core of the city.

The Sisters of Mercy established St. Mary's Hospital with 15 patient beds in the former McNamara home at 145 South Lafayette in 1893, in the heart of what has to become downtown Grand Rapids.

Five years later, medical education came to St. Mary's Hospital with the opening of a training school for nurses. The same year, 1898, saw the $10,000 construction of a three-story addition to the hospital, doubling the number of beds to 30.

Saint Mary's has always shown a real commitment to downtown Grand Rapids. For instance, the health care organization put new facilities in the Washington Square Urban Renewal Area in 1965 and in 1989 opened an HIV clinic in the poverty-stricken Heartside neighborhood on the south side of downtown Grand Rapids.

The Heartside neighborhood became a home for people thrown out of mental health institutions during the Reagan administration, as well as a home for the disenfranchised of the community, people who were and are truly unemployable.

That is still true. But, the Heartside neighborhood is also another example of the reinvention of Grand Rapids. An arts and entertainment community, Avenue for the Arts, is growing along the neighborhood's main thoroughfare, Division Avenue.

This is not the Grand Rapids that I made my adopted hometown in 1990. Pretty soon, it won't be the Grand Rapids I wrote about in 2012.

As the foundation was being laid for Van Andel Institute on the backbone of the Medical Mile, Michigan Street NE, Saint Mary's continued that urban commitment by launching three important construction projects: the Peter M. Wege Center for Health and Learning on the St. Mary's downtown campus, the Clinica Santa Maria in one of Grand Rapids' Hispanic neighborhoods on the southeast side of the city and the Browning Claytor Health Center the following year in one of the core city neighborhoods, the inner city of Grand Rapids.

One year before Phil McCorkle left his position at Spectrum-Butterworth to become president and CEO of Saint Mary's Health Care in 2000, and just as the anchor institutions were hitting full stride on Medical Mile, St. Mary's received a $10 million challenge grant from the Lacks family to build a cancer hospital.

That might seem like the kind of competition that would break the back of the collaborative spirit of Medical Mile, but it was not. This was another lesson to be learned on the Medical Mile that should be transferred to the next cluster of prosperity. Competition combined with collaboration can make everyone stronger.

Indeed, it was followed in 2002, by a major Spectrum Health-Saint Mary's Health partnership for the purchase of West Michigan's first PET/CT scanner, In 2003, Saint Mary's opened the Hauenstein Parkinson's Center that would become an integral part of the Parkinson's research on the Medical Mile as we detailed in an earlier chapter.

Medical Mile was never a straight line. Even at the beginning; it went at a right angle straight to Saint Mary's. But the public's focus was on Spectrum Health and Van Andel Institute, with Saint Mary's fighting for attention and philanthropic largess.

"We have created our own little "Medical Mile," on a quarter of a mile right here," said McCorkle.

He also told me that in the beginning, there were discussions about building two major centers of health care in Grand Rapids. One would be on the Medical Mile. The other would be on the Saint Mary's campus.

"We gave Peter Secchia the opportunity to build the Secchia MSU

College of Human Medicine campus right across the street from Saint Mary's," said McCorkle. "We were toying with the concept."

But the Medical Mile got it. Saint Mary's did not.

As you will read in the next chapter, the MSU College of Human Medicine's Grand Rapids campus was built on Michigan Street as one of the prime anchors of Medical Mile. It is growing even larger, as this book is being written, by taking over the site of the former offices of The Grand Rapids Press.

They might have lost the chance to have a Big Ten university's footprint on their campus, but McCorkle still believes they have created a mini-Medical Mile on the south side of downtown Grand Rapids. While it may not be the center of prosperity that awoke Michigan Street NE from its decades-long slumber, Saint Mary's has created its own healthcare community that serves as both a compliment and an alternative to the Medical Mile.

This campus includes new professional office buildings and Mary Free Bed Hospital, which is adjacent to the Saint Mary's facilities, along with the Heart of the City health clinic, and the American Cancer Society Hope Lodge.

One of the most important developments on the Saint Mary's campus came in late 2011 with the opening of a 6,000-square foot, eight-bed Clinical Trial Unit. This is West Michigan's first Clinical Trials Unit, opening with Phase 2 and Phase 3 clinical trials. Phase One trials were expected to follow shortly, according to a Saint Mary's announcement.

The Clinical Trial Unit consists of two separate components that each have four-bed modules. Research participants can stay overnight or even longer. One half of the unit includes specific security and safety features that allow CNS (central nervous system) clinical trials to be conducted. The other half of the unit focuses on non-CNS therapeutic areas which include, but are not limited to, oncology, diabetes, nephrology, and HIV/AIDS.

Clinical trials are so important to researchers on and off the Medical Mile. This is an absolutely necessity for the testing of new drugs and therapies. Top researchers would never come to a health care cluster that couldn't provide that.

It also gives researchers on Michigan Street NE one more reason to collaborate with Saint Mary's.

"While we don't have the MSU College of Human Medicine and Van Andel Research Institute, we have a strong presence ourselves," he said. "So, you can see we are doing something similar, maybe on a different scale."

What McCorkle said next, puts into two sentences what is one of the collateral benefits of the Medical Mile in Grand Rapids. In a very few words, it tells us why Grand Rapids and every city on the map needs to be in a state of constant reinvention.

"It (the Medical Mile) caused us to think very broadly and think of possibilities of what we can do," he explained. "You know, it was out-of-the-box thinking."

That could be the most important lesson to be learned from the Medical Mile. Grand Rapids has never shied away from reinvention. That is what is making Grand Rapids so different from the city I settled into in 1990. It is what is keeping the heart of Michigan Street NE beating. Opening our minds broke down the figurative Great Wall of Grand Rapids that served as a philosophic barrier to new money, new people, and new thoughts.

It is working on the Saint Mary's campus just as it is working on the Mile. "People are approaching us about wanting to join our medical staff," said McCorkle. "The people we are recruiting are looking for nice facilities, they want to participate in teaching activity, and a lot of them like to do research." They are finding that at Saint Mary's and at Spectrum Health, MSU and the VARI on the Medical Mile, all on a straight line with a jog south.

He foresees more development of the MSU College of Human Medicine and Van Andel Research Institute. As that happens, more international leaders will be coming to work in these centers of excellence. This is not just going to happen because of the individual institutions. McCorkle believes it is the partnerships and collaborations that are creating this new generation of health care in Grand Rapids.

"We will all reinforce the delivery of medical care together."

"Together" is the most important takeaway in that sentence. Together, the Medical Mile was built. Together it is growing. Together the health care and life sciences research communities are changing Grand Rapids.

The Saint Mary's Health Care Hauenstein Center is a perfect example of what is being made possible by the collaboration on Medical Mile, even though Saint Mary's is not geographically on what we think of as "The Mile."

Beyond the implications of the medical research being conducted at the Hauenstein Center, the complex is having a definite impact on the Grand Rapids community.

The economic ripple of the Center goes beyond the 173 jobs it created or the $12.4 million in new wages and salaries that would be pumped into the local economy.

W. E. Upjohn Institute for Employment Research Economist George Erickcek forecast in his 2006 study of the Hauenstein Center that the Center would have a much greater "per-employee economic impact" than other service providing industries because medical services not currently offered in the Grand Rapids area would now be available.[17]

That is a real bonus in the minds of economic developers because it means the Hauenstein Center is pulling in money that would have gone outside of the Grand Rapids area, making the effective employment multiplier for the Center 2.66 rather than the .97 generated by the average professional or technical services company.

This could be the impact of every institution on the Medical Mile. If they do attract patients, students, researchers, and scientists from outside the West Michigan region, providing services that are new to Grand Rapids; they could have the same multiplier effect. Every job created on the Mile could echo into nearly three more jobs created in the region.

The Hauenstein Center is named for a man who crafted and engineered one of the greatest lies ever told. Wall Street scammer Bernie Madoff should be envious of retired U.S. Army Col. Ralph Hauenstein because it was this Fort Wayne, Indiana native who was destined to stand at General Dwight Eisenhower's side in 1944, creating a diversion ---a lie -- that convinced Adolf Hitler the D-Day invasion was not going to

---

17   George Erickcek, *The Economic Impact of Saint Mary's Hauenstein Center on the Grand Rapids Area*, W.E. Upjohn Institute for Employment Research, 2006, 3-5

happen where Allied landing crafts unloaded the troops that helped to liberate France.

Hauenstein told me about the plan that included finding the body of an upper middle-class Englishman, dressing the corpse in a British uniform, loading it with phony maps and other false information and then parachuting it where German troops were sure to find the body.

He also created a fake air base complete with rubber aircraft and mannequins that were moved around every night so that it would look like an active military installation when German spy planes flew over the island the next day.

Ralph also told me how to make sure the perfect lie works. First, make sure that you are telling your victim what he wants to hear. Second, it helps if that victim is surrounded with 'yes men' who will back up whatever he wants to believe. Hitler wanted to believe, his officers wanted to make him happy. Hitler believed.

There was no scam in the creation of the Hauenstein Center. It is closely partnered with Van Andel Institute and the Michigan State University College of Human Medicine in the investigation of the cause and cure for Parkinson's disease.

The Hauenstein Center is a $60 million facility that includes neuroscience clinics involved in Alzheimer's, epilepsy, spine, stroke, neurosurgery and Parkinson's research. Saint Mary's also included a new emergency room and a critical care unit in the complex on the southeast side of downtown Grand Rapids.

Hauenstein donated $2 million to the $15 million campaign to create the Center that bears his name. That was not unusual. Just as philanthropy and public service have always been a part of the Grand Rapids culture, they are engrained in the DNA of this former Grand Rapids Herald editor.

Perhaps Parkinson's disease is one of the great uniting forces of the Medical Mile. Just as was the case with Dave Van Andel and Dr. Patrik Brundin, Ralph Hauenstein's father was killed by Parkinson's. Ralph's wife, Grace died of Alzheimer's.

Now Van Andel, Brundin and Hauenstein are leading the fight to conquer those diseases on the Medical Mile.

McCorkle remembered talking to Hauenstein about Parkinson's research when they opened a small clinic in an office building adjacent to Saint Mary's hospital. He told Hauenstein that it would be too small. They needed to build something bigger. Ralph's reply: "Let's do it." [18]

They did it. But they did not do it alone. The Hauenstein Center, like everything else in this new Grand Rapids-West Michigan health care community is a partnership. That partnership includes Michigan State University College of Human Medicine.

---

18   Pat Shellenbarger, "New Hauenstein Center at Saint Mary's Health Care, M-Live *The Grand Rapids Press,* Feb. 14, 2009. Accessed April 12, 2012. http://www.mlive.com/news/grand-rapids/index.ssf/2009/02/new_hauenstein_center_at_st_ma.html

Chapter Thirteen:
Growing Doctors

Grand Rapids needed more doctors in the late 19th century. But unlike the 21st century, this wasn't something they could import. Our ancestors were nowhere near as mobile as we are. Even if Grand Rapids could be marketed as a destination community, how were they going to get the new doctors here? The closest thing they had to an expressway system was the Grand River. No problem. The medical community just grew its own.

The first attempt to create a physician community didn't go well. Grand Rapids Medical College opened its doors in 1897, organized by a group of local physicians who became its faculty. They offered a three-year program, as well as a six-month course in veterinary medicine.

This worked out better for the animals than the people living in Grand Rapids. They did manage to graduate some veterinary students in 1898, but no medical doctors. The school closed because of a scandal.

No problem. Grand Rapids is all about reinvention. The medical school reopened the following year and graduated 108 students some of whom became highly respected doctors in the community.

However, the school closed down for good in 1906 under pressure from a much-better four-year program that the University of Michigan was running.

Maybe that was a good thing, based on the 1905 Grand Rapids Medical College class yell:

"Well man, sick man, dead man stiff!
Dig 'em up, cut 'em up, what's the diff?
Humorous, tumorous, Dead or alive,
Grand Rapids Medics 1905."[19]

---

19   Z.Z. Lydens, editor, *The Story of Grand Rapids*, (Grand Rapids: Kregel

Its confidence or maybe its desperation not shaken by that class yell, Grand Rapids did grow its own doctors. Bedside manner aside, some of these doctors did the kind of research that foreshadowed what would come on Medical Mile. Men like Dr. Schuyler Graves. This Grand Rapids physician was trying to figure out what to do about appendicitis ten years before the Class of '05 graduated.

Graves investigated 25 cases of the disease. He operated on 12 of the patients. Six died. The doctor treated the rest medically and four died. He concluded that appendicitis was a dangerous disease.

Before Dr. Graves, there was Dr. Van Noorden. He created a special diet for diabetics in 1899: 100 grams of oatmeal, 100 grams of eggs, 300 grams of butter that was all cooked together and divided five ways. As one newspaper reporter wrote at the time, "the only saving grace was the addition of eight ounces of coffee and one of whiskey."[20]

This is a different day and a different century, but we still have the same attitude in Grand Rapids. We want more doctors and health care professionals. Because Grand Rapids was not yet a destination community in the first years of the 21st century, Grand Rapids again decided to grow its own.

The people who put the Medical Mile together also realized that to make Grand Rapids a destination city for the best in medicine, Michigan Street NE had to have a world-renowned medical school.

That was a given. To grow and attract a new medical community, the Medical Mile had to have a medical school. Here was another given: Grand Rapids is overwhelmingly Spartan Green. Civic and community leaders agreed that they would do whatever it took to bring the MSU College of Human Medicine from its home in East Lansing to Grand Rapids early in their discussions of creating the Medical Mile.

It took millions of dollars and who knows how many man and woman hours, but it worked. The Michigan State University College of Human Medicine is an integral part of Medical Mile.

An open question though is why the University of Michigan didn't fight harder to become a stronger presence on the Medical Mile. Why did U-M cede the education pillar of Michigan Street NE to MSU?

Bringing the MSU College of Human Medicine to the Mile was about

Publications, 1966), 514

20   Z.Z. Lydens, editor, *The Story of Grand Rapids,* (Grand Rapids: Kregel Publications, 1966), 366-377

more than growing doctors and nurses, scientists and researchers. As with everything on Medical Mile, we are hoping it will be help keep our children close to home, or at least bring them back once they do leave. There is nothing wrong with scoring on the rebound.

Michigan media called it the "brain drain." A century after the class of 1905 left Grand Rapids Medical College, U.S. Census Bureau numbers showed us that more than half of Michigan's college and university graduates had left the state. It was our future leaving Michigan.

To borrow a phrase and a theme from former President Bill Clinton's book, "Back to Work," Medical Mile is about building a new future for Grand Rapids by creating a cluster of prosperity. We have decided that keeping our young people close to home is at least as important as attracting new brainpower to West Michigan.

We spent the single digit years of the new century trying to figure out why our kids hated us, reading books like *The Rise of the Creative Class*, by Richard Florida, assuming at first that our communities in Michigan just were not hip enough, that we were not friendly enough, not diverse enough.

However, I really think that was, and is, a symptom of the real problem. Our children just did not see a future for themselves in Michigan. To tell you the truth, neither did we. Here is the thing: There were no jobs in Michigan, at least not enough.

The Michigan State University College of Human Medicine and the Medical Mile are helping to change the perception that became reality.

Take for instance, Alex Gilde. He is a big, broad-shouldered, blond-haired, blue-eyed, guy who grew up shoveling gravel at his family's cement company. He started shoveling on his 12th birthday and kept slinging gravel until he moved to Grand Rapids and started classes at Grand Valley State University.

It gave Alex a strong back, thick shoulders and "a great motivation to get an education," he told me as we had coffee together at Bagel Beanery at the east end of Medical Mile.

Now he is an M.D. candidate at the MSU College of Human Medicine with a B.S. in biomedical sciences.

Dr. Sarah Mattson was in the first group to come to the MSU College of Human Medicine as part of a pre-clinical rotation. She was one of the pioneering students on Medical Mile.

Her first years in Grand Rapids were in a temporary building just south of the permanent MSU campus. "We were close enough to watch it going up as we went to class," she remembered. "Then we got to go to one of the luncheons to thank the construction workers."

The MSU College of Human Medicine, founded in 1964 on the Michigan State University campus in East Lansing, moved to Grand Rapids' Medical Mile as the result of a community initiative led by, among others, MSU alum, Peter Secchia.

The Medical Mile-MSU campus is named "The Secchia Center" in recognition of a gift from the former U.S. Ambassador to Italy that will total $20 million toward the $40 million in private support that was required to complete the project. Rich and Helen DeVos announced a $5 million matching grant campaign in 2010 to help raise the money needed to finish the construction. The Steelcase Foundation and Frey Foundation contributed $1 million each to the MSU College of Human Medicine, funds that supported construction of the Secchia Center.

What did we learn from this?

This is a classic example of Grand Rapids' "damn the recession attitude" that put enough building cranes in the skies of the community to attract national attention at a time when America's economy seemed to have hit rock bottom post -2008.

It is also an example of the "those who have are those who give" attitude. Grand Rapids is much more fortunate that the rest of Michigan because old money is staying close to home, and investing in their hometown.

It had also better drive home the point that we need to be growing another generation of philanthropists who will share the Medical Mile dream and help build the next cluster of prosperity.

First and second-year students attend classes at either the $90 million Secchia Center in Grand Rapids or on the MSU campus in East Lansing. During the third and fourth years of the program, they complete a series of required and elective clerkships at one of MSU's seven community-based program sites in Flint, Grand Rapids, Kalamazoo, Lansing, Midland, Traverse City, and Michigan's Upper Peninsula.

The college planned to enroll its inaugural class of 100 first-year students in Grand Rapids in 2010, when the new facility opened. Once the program is at full capacity, enrollment in Grand Rapids will be approximately 350 students.

They were already looking to more than double that to 800, as this book went to press.

Six Grand Valley State University pre-med students, including Alex, made up the first group to be admitted to the Michigan State University College of Human Medicine through an agreement that was signed in 2011 by the two universities.

Grand Valley and MSU created the Early Assurance Program that links pre-med GVSU students to MSU's College of Human Medicine. It gives Alex, his classmates, and other qualified pre-med students who wish to practice in underserved areas a head start toward admission.

It has since been extended to most of the other colleges in the Grand Rapids area, serving as another example of the collaboration that is driving the Medical Mile. The phrase "practice in underserved areas" is also an important indicator of the recognition of the real mission on the Mile.

Alex enrolled at GVSU to play football, and get a little bit of academic money by playing nose tackle for three years. His football career and the injuries that went along with it also gave Alex a real affinity for orthopedics. He was thinking that would be his specialty when we met at Bagel Beanery.

He gives us hope for the future of Grand Rapids. Not only did Alex transfer from GVSU to MSU in the first class of their shared early-admittance program, he actually bought a house in Grand Rapids.

"Been there (in his home) for a year and a half, six years in Grand Rapids and I am thinking now that I will do my residency here and practice here." Bingo! That is just what the people who created Medical Mile want to hear. The brain drain can be plugged.

Alex also told me he was attracted to Grand Rapids by more than just the MSU College of Human Medicine. This team player likes the team on Medical Mile.

"There is a decent integration between Michigan State and the hospital, and access to some of the faculty members," he explained. "I have been doing research with a doctor in the Musculoskeletal Center at Spectrum."

Once students get into their clinical rotation they can go to Spectrum and/or Saint Mary's. So again it is that one-stop shopping that comes with a billion-dollar campus.

"We obviously have very strong partnerships with Van Andel Institute, Saint Mary's Health Care, and Spectrum Health and we can see all of those partners from our balcony," MSU College of Human Medicine Dean Marsha Rappley told me in her office inside the Secchia Center on the Medical Mile. "I think that sends a very strong message to our students, our faculty and I hope to the community about how our futures are so tied together."

Even though her first years on Medical Mile were in the formative period of the campus, Dr. Mattson also believes it was real bonus to be part of the Mile.

"We could go up to the (Spectrum-Butterworth) hospital, we could study up there, and now as a resident it all goes backwards. I still have the medical school that is accessible to me as a resident," Sarah explained. "I think it gives you a focus. We know that all of this is dedicated to one thing."

She was doing her residency in obstetrics-gynecology when I talked to her at a coffee shop in Cascade Township, one of the higher-end suburbs in the outer rings around Grand Rapids.

The mother of two, her second baby was born just weeks before we met, was very excited about the future, which she and her husband both see as being centered in Grand Rapids. Sarah was convinced that she had made the right choice for her specialty and equally convinced that it was her experience on the Mile that led her to this path.

This is not what she had planned. The OB-GYN life is notoriously hard and all consuming. Originally, Dr. Mattson did not want to do what she wound up doing. The Mile gets all of the credit for changing her mind.

"My very first day in the hospital, my very first rotation, I went in to do a gynecologic surgery and I came out of there and I was like, 'This is it. This is absolutely it,'" she remembered. "Every single day of that rotation was just…I absolutely loved it."

She and her husband are both from the Grand Rapids area. But after high school neither wanted to stay here. He is from Rockford, she is from Greenville and both moved out west for their first two years of college before rebounding back to West Michigan.

Even after graduating from GVSU, Sarah had her bags packed. Dr. Mattson looked at 15 other schools before deciding to become a Spartan on the MSU College of Human Medicine campus.

"I really think this (Grand Rapids) is an undiscovered gem. The places that were bigger, that I thought would have more opportunities, really didn't have more opportunities," she said. "It was a surprise to me. I think a lot of people don't realize how much we have here."

Sarah and Alex want to be here. The Grand Rapids community wants them here. Dr. Rappley told me that makes a big difference for her school and her students.

"The students don't really get it because they have not been out at other medical schools yet," said Dr. Rappley. "In other places, medical students are not very well respected. They are at the bottom of the totem pole."

Grand Rapids is different. "Here they are very much welcomed. People talk to them about building careers in this place. They are respected in a way that is quite unusual."

It is true that while Grand Rapids is not a college town, it is certainly a town of colleges. Grand Valley State University, Grand Rapids Community College, Aquinas College, Kendall College, Ferris State University, University of Michigan, Western Michigan University, Hope College, Cornerstone University, and Davenport University all have a presence in the Grand Rapids metropolitan area.

Does that make Grand Rapids above average? Is that the secret to the success of Medical Mile? Not really. This town of colleges is not all that unusual. If you take away Medical Mile, there are plenty of large metro areas that have any number of higher educational institutions.

However, Dr. Rappley said there is a difference in Grand Rapids that gave Michigan State University an advantage and a head-start in making this partnership as part of Medical Mile work.

"It is remarkable how the institutions are respectful of one another and how the community feels a real ownership of these institutions," she said.

Dr. Mattson does get it. "We have so much dedication from the people in the community that want to make this better. They put a lot of money and effort into developing our education. All of that is kind of under the radar," she told me. "I don't think you see it as much until you are in it."

It is the level and unanimity of support that Dr. Rappley found surprising. She also pointed out what we in Grand Rapids have always seen as self-evident. Those with money, give money. Tithing is part of the culture.

"But beyond that it is sort of the moral support saying, 'you are part of our future, and we want our children to have these wonderful opportunities of education," Dr. Rappley explained.

We had a very pleasant conversation until I brought up the question of Western Michigan University in Kalamazoo setting up its own medical school. That is when the conversation turned a little frosty.

"It is already displacing our students," she said. "We had planned to place 40 students a year here. We won't be able to do that. It has definitely caused us to organize in different ways."

While everyone is more than willing to talk about the spirit of collaboration for the common good on Medical Mile, there is still competition on the Mile and beyond. There is a fine line between collaboration and competition.

Does Dr. Rappley at least wish Western Michigan University well? "They are good people, so ...yeah."

She feels much better about another university that is a major player on Medical Mile and even a more important force in the reinvention of this American community, Grand Valley State University.

Chapter Fourteen:
Tearing Down Fences

Joyce Johnson is a Grand Rapids Central High School student working part-time at Saint Mary's Hospital earning close to $12 an hour, setting up and breaking down patient rooms because of what she learned in her classes inside the Grand Valley State University Cook-DeVos Center for Health Sciences on Medical Mile.

Planning to go to Grand Valley State University to study pre-med, Joyce, her friends call her J.J., was also looking forward to shadowing a 4th or 5th year MSU College of Human Medicine student a fewer hours after we met in her classroom

J.J. is also going to be the first person in her family to graduate from high school.

Purpose and confidence shine through the eyes of this African American teenager as she tells you her plans for life and asks, "What motivates you?"

My answer didn't come close to matching hers.

J.J. watched her uncle's wife, April, die of cancer in 2005, "...my heart was falling to pieces. "This was so unbearable," J.J. wrote in her application to become part of a Kent Intermediate School District program on Medical Mile. "I still haven't gotten over the fact that I couldn't help at all."

"Eli" is one of J.J's classmates. He didn't plan to ever again sit in a classroom after high school. But a librarian suggested that Eli get involved in architectural engineering. That led him to the KISD Health, Science and Technology program at Grand Rapids Central High.

"It became a dream and then a goal for me," Eli wrote in his application. "Look at me now."

Eli, J.J. and their classmates are building a foundation in physics and chemistry. They also learn how to do bedside care, diagnostic testing and a blood draw. The idea is to give them a 360-degree view of health care.

That is what got J.J. ready to work at Saint Mary's.

"It is important for kids not to just understand theory. They need to understand relevant application," said KISD Director of Career Readiness Jarrad Grandy. "That is why they get the lab time, and beyond that they get into a work-based environment in the labs, with the scientists."

J.J. and Eli are not only getting practical, hands-on lab experience, and a top-notch health sciences education, they are also earning college credits.

When it is all said and done they could have 12-to-14 transcripted college credits, not articulated, at no-cost.

Grandy and I met in the lobby of the GVSU-CHS building, surrounded by high school and college students on their lunch hour, each competing to be heard over the other in a cacophony of voices that is an expression of the energy radiating inside this five-story building that is one of the anchors of the Medical Mile.

The GVSU Cook-DeVos Center for Health Sciences is a dream factory. High school students, college undergraduates and grad students, scientists, researchers, entrepreneurs are all mixing, mingling, learning and dreaming together.

The college students are either bused, or drive, in from the Grand Valley State University campus in suburban Allendale. The high school and Grand Rapids Community College students usually walk, slipping and sliding up the steep, icy hill that Michigan Street NE becomes in the winter and then back down again at the end of the day.

Spring and summer are different. That is when you see these students in small groups, kicking their shoes off, reading, learning and doing their dreaming outside on Michigan Street.

The flow of students to and from the GVSU-CHS building never stops. There is also a flow of traffic making left and right turns at Michigan and Lafayette as their teachers enter the building from the other side. Entrepreneurs who are building new businesses on the fifth-floor park beside them and join the flow from the parking garage at the rear of the building.

They all come together in the lobby. Students looking for direction, teachers leading them, small business owners and small business dreamers; they all come together at the Center for Health Sciences.

The interaction and mentoring made possible by the billion-dollar

Medical Mile campus allows students to work with some of the best minds on the globe. "And those relationships are only going to get deeper in the next year," said Grandy, as more bureaucratic fences are torn down.

Kent Intermediate School District and Grand Rapids Public Schools administrators did not waste any time putting this program together. The discussion of how they could work together to better prepare students for careers in health sciences was a parallel conversation to the construction of Medical Mile.

This is another lesson taught on the Medical Mile: the lesson of parallel opportunities.

"Would our program be as large as it now without Medical Mile?" asked Grandy. "No. There is no way that could happen."

It happened because Grand Valley State University's administration and board saw the Medical Mile as an opportunity for the school that moved from the Ottawa County countryside into the city and became a major player in the reinvention of Grand Rapids.

Rich DeVos, Jay Van Andel, Peter Cook, Peter Secchia, and more all played a large role in creating Medical Mile and not coincidentally, a new Grand Rapids. However, I really believe that the Grand Rapids I live in today is not the city I moved into in 1990 because of what Grand Valley State University has done in the city's downtown district.

GVSU is not the only institution of higher education in downtown Grand Rapids. But Grand Valley State University is the big money.

GVSU is the second-largest investor in the new downtown Grand Rapids, trailing only the medical community. The university has invested $150 million in its downtown campuses; the Eberhard Center, the Pew Campus and the Cook-DeVos Center for Health Sciences, which is one of the anchor buildings on Medical Mile. Another $40 million investment is on the way with the new Seidman School of Business facility that will be built on the school's ever-expanding downtown campus.

Has this been good for Grand Rapids? "Look at downtown and compare it to any other downtown in Michigan, save Ann Arbor where the U-of-M central campus now occupies most of the central core," GVSU Vice President Matt McLogan said during a meeting on the GVSU Pew Campus in downtown Grand Rapids.

"It is education. It is health. It is law. It is finance. Not only has this kept downtown Grand Rapids viable, it has grown and it is growing still.

I don't believe there is another downtown in Michigan that can make that statement."

There is no denying McLogan's point.

When you stand at the top of the GVSU Cook-DeVos Center for Health Sciences staircase and look out the front window that goes from its fifth-floor ceiling to the street below, you can see the Heritage Hill neighborhood to the south of Medical Mile, the neighborhood that J.J walks through to get to the CHS building.

Ten-thousand people to a square mile, some big, old wood frame homes, some brick, many of them former mansions, purchased and renovated in the 1960s and '70s, rescued from the urban revitalization that bulldozed much of the city's history.

If you turn away from the windows and focus inside the CHS building, you will see everything that could be the future of Grand Rapids, thanks to Medical Mile. The building pulsates with the energy of young people, high school and college students, studying the allied or non-doctor health professions, working side-by-side with doctors, nurses, researchers and life sciences entrepreneurs.

In other words, the GVSU Cook-DeVos Center for Health Sciences is filled with dreams. Isn't that what Medical Mile is all about?

It is all about the dream that "it will get better" as Jay Van Andel and Rich DeVos learned from their parents and taught their children. This is also about the dream that every parent has; the dream that their children's lives will be better than theirs.

This is also where Grand Valley State University is teaching the next wave of allied health professionals who are going to be our health technicians, our nurses, and the people behind the scenes.

Some of these GVSU students on Medical Mile are earning their RN/BSN degrees. Others are working on their Master of Science in Nursing or Doctor of Nursing degrees at the GVSU Kirkhof College of Nursing on the third floor of the CHS building.

Kirkhof College is part of the educational community quilt in Grand Rapids and Dean Cynthia McCurren, Ph.D., RN told me that Grand Valley State University is using its location on Medical Mile as an opportunity to contribute to the community, to help make Grand Rapids a better place. It is all part of the Kirkhof experience in which her students are immersed.

"They are learning very important skills and are actually contributing to the community at the same time," Dr. McCurren said. "We are making a difference."

She echoed the spirit of continual collaboration that is espoused in the administrative offices and C-suites on Medical Mile, telling me that she has been very intentional about seeking out an understanding of what Kirkhof College can do for Spectrum Health.

That goes both ways. Kirkhof faculty members serve on Spectrum committees and a Spectrum representative sits on the Kirkhof board.

Why couldn't this kind of collaboration we are seeing on Medical Mile, the breaking down of institutional borders, this cross-pollination of principles and ideals, serve as a model for the health care reform that seems to be limping across the U.S. as this book is being written?

It should certainly serve as a model for the evolution of the Mile along with the creation of the next cluster of prosperity in Grand Rapids.

McCurren believes we are at a "real tipping point" for what needs to happen across the spectrum of health care delivery systems and education.

"In order to deliver patient-centered care and close gaps in that care, we together need to understand how to solve those problems instead of educating in silos," McCurren said during our phone conversation. "Moving out of silos is what is happening on Medical Mile."

She said the "proximity" of working virtually in each other's laps on Medical Mile has helped to break down those barriers. However it takes more than that. This has to be done on purpose. As McCurren said, it has to be intentional.

Dean McCurren rides high on the Medical Mile learning curve with that thought. We must continue to break down barriers and tear down the fences that were the boundaries of our old way of thinking.

The fence that kept high school students away from their college counterparts has been torn down on the Medical Mile. Thanks to a Kent Intermediate School District (KISD) program and cooperation of higher education administrators in Grand Rapids, high school students, like J.J. are rubbing shoulders, sharing thoughts and shadowing the people they dream of becoming.

GVSU President Emeritus Arend (Don) Lubbers told me over lunch that he decided to build a downtown Grand Rapids campus during the recession of the mid-1970s. Like any good CEO of that time, he wanted to be ready for life after the recession.

"It was one of the most enjoyable, interesting, political times in my career. We decided in 1976 that a downtown campus would be a good thing. It took us to 1988 to get it."

Lubbers felt GVSU had to be on Medical Mile as soon as he heard about the concept.

"We had brought some of our health programs downtown. They were growing and we could see that was going to be a big part of the future. So as we started talking about Medical Mile, I thought 'boy, Grand Valley had better be a part of that.'"

In the mid to late 1990s, the GVSU Allied Health programs in Henry Hall on the Allendale campus were completely out of room, even though they were only a few years old.

Like just about everything in Grand Rapids during those years, it was time for a re-set. It was time for some fresh and critical thinking. McLogan said they were looking at grafting the Allied Health space next to the university's Eberhard Center or the GVSU Seidman School of Business on the school's Pew campus, both of which are in downtown Grand Rapids.

Lubbers remembered sending McLogan on a search-and-discover mission to find GVSU a space on Medical Mile. At the same time, McLogan said he was already "walking the property and looking up on the (Michigan Street) Hill wondering, 'why surround these health students with business students, let's see if we can find a space to put it up on the Hill near the hospital.'"

McLogan knew that Spectrum Health had just acquired a piece of property at Michigan Street and Lafayette Avenue that he thought would be perfect for GVSU.

He presented the concept to Spectrum officials, "There were two ways for this to go at the end of that meeting," McLogan remembered. "The expected one was, 'we just bought this property for ourselves, nice talking to you, so long.' The other one was 'let's continue talking.'"

They kept talking. The discussions continued. In less than three months, GVSU had an agreement to purchase the land from Spectrum. That gave the university the footprint it needed on Medical Mile for the Cook-DeVos Center for Health Sciences.

"Bud Sherwood was the chair of the hospital's holding company and he has always been a friend to Grand Valley, so he really helped us," said Lubbers. "If it had been someone else, I don't think they ever would have sold the land."

"It is helpful to have friends in places that are important to you."

In the Old World way that universities purchased property, GVSU had to actually own the land before asking the state (of Michigan) for assistance to construct the CHS building.

It took another year-and-a-half to get the proposal through the state legislative process. In 1998, it was approved, then after another year of planning, the building opened for the 2002-03 academic year.

"Things do not usually go that quickly in higher education construction," McLogan explained. One GVSU project during his time at the school had taken several years to move forward and another that had taken 15 years.

The CHS project, really everything on the Medical Mile, might never have happened, if it had been put off until the 21st century. McLogan believes this came together because it happened, "pre-term limits (in the Michigan Legislature), when there were still legislators who understood the implications of what they were doing and would be around to see the fulfillment of what they had done."

The Medical Mile's development might also have been hindered by the attitude that governments should never get into the business of picking winners and losers in the public or private sectors.

McLogan does not believe the Engler administration or the Legislature stepped over that ideological line. He said the GVSU move to Medical Mile was guided by private investment and free-market thought.

"We took considerable comfort in the fact that Blodgett, Butterworth, Spectrum, Saint Mary's, Mary Free Bed and Metro (hospitals)," all had expansion plans on the board or underway," he explained. "That confirmed our judgment that the Allied Health field would continue to be very important."

GVSU administrators and trustees made a clear decision they did not want to open a medical college, but would instead focus on the allied health fields. "In effect, that opened the door to Michigan State University or some other medical school entity with an interest in Grand Rapids," said McLogan

That is not to say GVSU did not give serious consideration to opening up a medical school. They did. But McLogan said they decided to stick with what they were doing, what they felt they were doing very well.

"We are the region's largest provider of non-doctor medical personal, so we decided to just keep on doing what we do well," he stated. "We expand those programs when the medical community identifies a need for a profession that is non-doctor."

How is that working out for them? It is going much better than expected. The Cook-DeVos Center, as this book was written, was "full to the rafters and we are turning away wonderfully qualified people because we don't have room," said McLogan. GVSU was laying plans to build again on Medical Mile, a 1.6 acre, $3.25 million parcel of land adjacent to the Cook-DeVos CHS, as he and I met.

In the next decade, McLogan said university officials expect to create labs and classrooms in that new building, staying on mission, staying on point, continuing to work to identify what the medical community needs in terms of health care professionals.

In a word, GVSU has the same mission in the Center for Health Sciences as does Grand Rapids Community College, Grand Rapids Public Schools and the Kent Intermediate School District and that word is: Reinvention.

There is one more entity in the GVSU Cook-DeVos Center for Health Sciences that is all about invention and re-invention, the West Michigan Technology and Science Initiative.

CHAPTER FIFTEEN:
Where Dreams Begin

"WE CERTAINLY WOULD NOT be in business as vigorously as we are today without WMTSI," said Syzgy Biotech Solutions CEO Barry Nowak. "This environment is like nitrogen for growing biotech businesses." [21]

Ideas, money and opportunity are coming together on the top floor of the Grand Valley State University Cook-DeVos Center for Health Sciences (CHS). The high school and college students we met in the last chapter are not the only residents of this building on the north side of Michigan Street NE. This is also where the West Michigan Science and Technology Initiative (WMSTI) is incubating new entrepreneurs whose inventions could save our lives and make them millionaires.

There is no need to be embarrassed about that. We want to make Medical Mile millionaires who will reinvest their profits in Grand Rapids, whether they chose the Mile or the next cluster of prosperity. That is a lesson that needs to be learned and transferred.

But, the immediate concern is growing the next generation of techno-preneurs, the technology entrepreneurs who will take Medical Mile to the next stage and/or grow the next cluster of prosperity, another pod of innovation that will burst open with ideas.

The dream is that this WMSTI space will turn out to be a 21st century, Grand Rapids, Mich. version of Thomas Edison's two-city block long invention center in Menlo Park, New Jersey. That was dedicated to creating inventions that would change the lives of Americans and be affordable to even the most average among our ancestors.

---

21   Kym Reinstadler, "From the attic to the lab. Syzgy again successful in securing funds for startup 'hillbilly biotech firm.' MiBiz July 7, 2011. Accessed April 13, 2012

Rod Kackley

The GVSU Cook-DeVos CHS fifth floor is also home to the West Michigan Medical Device Consortium, which serves as a trade organization and hopefully a magnet to attract medical device makers to Grand Rapids.

Medical device manufacturing or medical technology could really be a bonanza for West Michigan. We already have one of the biggest global players headquartered about an hour south of Grand Rapids, in Kalamazoo.

Stryker Corp. was launched by a University of Michigan trained physician in the basement of Kalamazoo's Borgess Hospital in 1936. It was the 12th largest medical technology company in the world in 2010, with total estimated sales of more than $7.3 billion.

Its founder, Dr. Homer Stryker, is a West Michigan innovator who wound up striking it rich. He was an orthopedic surgeon who, when he could not find the equipment he needed, simply invented it.

Ever wonder why a doctor can use a saw to cut a cast cut off your arm without breaking the skin? He can do it because of Dr. Stryker's invention of an oscillating saw. The secret of oscillation came to him in a "late-night brainstorm" according to Stryker corporate literature that also tells us the prototype was powered by the motor from a malted milk mixer.

That is just what the Medical Mile needs, another late night brainstorm from another Homer Stryker. He, or she, might be on the fifth floor of the CHS building right now. Or he or she might be one of Eli's or J.J.'s classmates, or maybe a researcher across the street. In a few years we will find out.

"I think it takes about 40 years to create something like we are creating here. We got a jump start on that by about 10 years with the gift from the Van Andel family," said Rich Cook, WMSTI Venture Center Director, a tall, white-haired man who is a midwife for the entrepreneurs pregnant with new ideas.

His training is in physics, his hobby is alternative energy and Rich knows marketing very well, from both a corporate and global perspective. He knows how to find the real players with the real money and how to talk to them.

The West Michigan Science and Technology Initiative that opened in 2003 is also an example of the "public-private partnership" model that should be given credit for much of the economic development we have seen to date on the Mile; the construction, the jobs and the buildings bearing the names of those generous enough to send millions of the next generation's inheritance to philanthropic causes across Grand Rapids. Those families are part of the partnership.

The Mile shows Grand Rapids' real secret to success, a pairing of shared vision and money from the families of DeVos, Van Andel, Cook, Secchia, et.al. However, as powerful as they are, Grand Rapids' billionaires and millionaires did not do this alone. The public sector is as much a part of this as the private and philanthropic sectors.

The Michigan Economic Development Corp. (MEDC) powered by state tax dollars and armed with tax incentives, and the city of Grand Rapids are partnered with Van Andel Institute, Grand Valley State University, Grand Rapids Community College, and The Right Place Inc. as the guiding force, to drive the West Michigan Science and Technology Initiative.

WMSTI is in one of 15 "Smart Zones" established by Michigan officials with the intention of creating geographic clusters of innovation where technology-based firms and entrepreneurs could join forces to build our future.

Businesses located within the Zones can also take advantage of the Michigan Pre-Seed Capital Fund, opening the door to early-stage money needed to push the entrepreneurs' dreams to development and then to market.

The Smart Zones and the Pre-Seed Capital Fund are concentrated on advanced automotive, manufacturing and materials; alternative energy; homeland security and defense; and life sciences. It is the Tri-Technology Corridor established by former Gov. Jennifer Granholm, an expansion of former Gov. John Engler's Life Sciences Corridor.

The Grand Rapids Smart Zone includes two of those specialties, life sciences and medical device manufacturing, in its 26-thousand-square-foot CHS space. As this book went to press, there were five companies inside the Smart Zone, employing 41 people.

Rich Cook's job is to help them grow. He is their Father Goose.

"My mission, my entire life, has been to create globally competitive, technologically based products that result in jobs," he pauses and looks over the top of his glasses for both emphasis and assurance that I am paying attention, "good paying jobs, that will continue to reside here in West Michigan."

Cook can offer his WMSTI brood connections to power brokers and money. He can get entrepreneurs to the right people. "Access to capital is the second highest value I can provide, the third highest is coaching," he explained.

Rich does not share a concern commonly expressed about a lack of venture capital or angel money hindering the Medical Mile. The money is there. Entrepreneurs just need to develop a new skill set to find it.

"If an entrepreneur has a good idea and they can learn to express it well as a value proposition and if it is a good value proposition, they can find capital," he said. "They should be able to find it relatively quickly, within 6 to 9 months."

However, that is a learned skill set. Only three or four out of the 400+ businesses he has coached could accomplish that by themselves.

"They usually need help to learn how to approach people with money and put the investor's hat on to state their value proposition," he explained to me. "I have to get them out of the technical-push mindset into a market-pull mentality."

Rich loves what he does. He is incredibly enthusiastic leading me through the WMSTI research labs

Showing me a new microscope with joy stick controls on either side, he sat on the stool in front of it, looked into the microscope, grabbed the sticks and energetically moved them back and forth like a teenager who had just dropped his last quarter into a video game. Cook looked back over his shoulder, smiled, and said, "This is where your gaming skills really come into play."

Then there is the particle accelerator that looks like the washing machine. "You know how your washer can start walking if it gets off its base, this could do that too," said Rich. "But it spins so fast that if it did, it go right though this wall," showing me with his hands and arms what the impact would be like.

"So we hope it never does happen," looking back and chuckling to make sure I caught the joke.

Kim Bode was there at the beginning. She was WMSTI's first marketing director.

"It took us a good year to realize what we needed to focus on and what industries we were going to serve," Kim remembered.

WMSTI's first executive director, Matt Dugener, and Kim knew that the life sciences had to be the focus if WMSTI was to be in line with the rest of the Mile. But they felt that would not be enough, so they fell back on Grand Rapids' manufacturing legacy.

"We discovered that we could have a very strong presence in medical devices," Bode said. "We had such a strong manufacturing base. But it needed to morph and change. It just made sense to work with them and help them transition into medical devices."

Don Beery is continuing that effort, a couple of doors down the hall from Rich Cook's office. He is the director of West Michigan Medical Device Consortium (WMMDC).

Don brought more than two decades of private sector manufacturing experience with him, most of it in the automotive industry, along with an engineering degree from Michigan Technological University and an MBA from Western Michigan University in Kalamazoo, when he was hired in August 2011.

Beery wants Grand Rapids to become one of the top medical device manufacturing hubs in the U.S. standing alongside Minneapolis/St. Paul, San Diego and Boston. The payoff for Grand Rapids would be huge.

The medical device, or medical technology space, is a $98 billion a year industry that analysts believe will continue growing at a 6% annual pace, breaking $122 billion a year by 2013.

There were 365,000 people working in medical technology in 2007. They got paid, on average, an outstanding $60,000. That would be big money in Michigan.

Beery thinks it is entirely possible that West Michigan could get a bigger slice of that pie. He could be right. We have the brainpower.

Just look at the region. We already have one medical school, the Michigan State University College of Human Medicine, with a second one on the way at Western Michigan University in Kalamazoo. If you combine that institutional power with the business intelligence, manufacturing history and capabilities that are all part of the region's DNA, you have to ask yourself, "Why not?"

West Michigan knows how to invent and manufacture, or as Don put it, "we think it up and then we build it."

You can't ignore or discount Grand Rapids' history that is steeped in manufacturing innovation. New concepts in office furniture, high-tech auto mirrors and wind turbines have come out of the area. Why not medical devices?

There were a lot of West Michigan manufacturers, mainly auto supply chain people, who watched their revenue dry up as Detroit's auto plants were grinding to a halt, and investigated the possibilities offered by medical device manufacturing.

They discovered making medical devices is not an easy thing to do. It requires a different skill set, and as one local economist pointed out recently, given the resurgence of the Detroit Three, aren't we glad those medical device plans didn't work out so well?

But, there are medical device people in Grand Rapids who are doing it right. It is Beery's job to help them grow. As he explained it, there are plenty of organizations to help the guy fiddling with the next great idea in his garage. Beery is glad to assist that person where he can, but the WMMDC is really a trade organization meant to help medical device makers grow their revenue streams.

It will not be easy. "It will take time. It will take effort. It will take money," Beery said as he pointed out his office window overlooking Medical Mile. "But we have demonstrated before that we are willing to do that and we know how to do that."

He sees the public-private sector partnership model that rebuilt Grand Rapids 20 years ago –I have said it before and I will say it again, this is not the city I moved into in 1990—as being critical to moving the region into the Top Five for medical device manufacturing. "It is night and day in Grand Rapids," Beery said, "because some folks cared about it and invested their time, energy and money in it. I'm not so sure we can't pull it off."

Venture capital and angel investment money will be important and he said there is never enough of that to go around, although Beery added that he sees the situation improving.

He also sees great potential for the Grand Rapids community if the area can become a Top Five medical device maker because it is manufacturing. Nothing feeds the family like manufacturing. Factories are capital intensive, land intensive –that means tax revenue—and jobs that are high-skilled, high-wage positions.

Beery said medical device jobs have an incredible multiplier impact. They create more than 3.5 jobs for every medical device manufacturing position. The initial job pumps money into the economy, big time, with the average annual salary 22-percent higher than the typical job in Michigan.

However, as much as Medical Mile is about organic growth, creating, developing and monetizing home-cooking, Beery doesn't think that will be enough. He believes we are going to have to go out and convince one of the big players to move to our town, planting their flag here. "That is the kind of velocity we are going to need to go there (to the Top Five) in a reasonable amount of time."

Again, Beery asks, why not?

Indeed, why not? Grand Rapids knows how to design things, create things, make things and move them to market. What could possibly go wrong? How about this? We might have the same trouble attracting big medical device manufacturing as we have attracting top talent to life sciences.

Michigan is in the Rust Belt. It is not one of the top life sciences or medical device manufacturing states. Grand Rapids is not San Jose or Boston.

This is another lesson that was learned in the creation of the Medical Mile and one that is going to be critical to move the Mile forward. We have to do a much better job of explaining why that perception is nowhere close to reality. We have to tell the world why that is so wrong.

"I came out of 17 years in the auto industry," said Beery. "The people I worked with are anything but low tech. They are putting $30,000 products on the road that run for 10 years with very few problems."

Tom Howing, the head of New Product Development at the West Michigan medical device and direct-sales catalog company, MarketLab Inc. told me that he sees a real future in medical device manufacturing for West Michigan. "It falls back to what this community cut its teeth on more than a century ago," said Howing. "Now, it is just a matter of asking, 'How can we work together cooperatively?'"

Drawing large medical device makers or the best minds in that industry to West Michigan has to be part of the strategy, according to Howing. "I think the climate is getting better. Although we have some hurdles to clear, I think this area is very much primed for growth. All of the elements are here."

Howing also pointed out that the medical device industry is already growing in West Michigan. "Once you kind of lift the cover, you find there is a lot more activity than most people know about."

He said West Michigan is primed for expansion in medical device manufacturing like this. "We have so many folks coming out of the contract furniture industry, the auto industry and so many others, that the knowledge, craftsmanship and lead times are all there. It is just a matter of knowing who they are and how to connect with them."

This list does not include companies that are abandoning their core competencies. These are businesses that "are very much expanding," according to Howing. "I think when the market took a turn for the worse they were all looking to diversify."

It seemed like he was getting a call a week from someone saying, "We are really strong in automotive, but we really want to get into health care.

If I had a dollar for every time someone said that," Howing said. "But the reality was they had the skill sets, the equipment and the talent to do it."

We make cars in Michigan. We make a lot of cars. And what is a car? It is a computer with four wheels, and even though we do hear about auto industry recalls, doesn't your car work better than your laptop? Imagine restarting your car as often as you reboot your computer.

Michigan and Grand Rapids are loaded with high-skilled, high-tech people in the automotive and furniture manufacturing communities, just the kind of people that have to be very attractive to the big medical device companies.

But are there enough of them? That is something that scares Beery. It is not just here in Grand Rapids. One of the biggest problems facing manufacturing across the U.S. today is a lack of talent. But it really isn't a new challenge. It has been a pressing concern in manufacturing for years. For a lot of reasons, we skipped a whole generation of workers in our factories.

Today, I still have to write that there are far too few engineers and manufacturing is even more desperate to find them. One West Michigan manufacturer told me in January 2012 that an engineering student just out of school could write his or her own ticket.

That is just what could derail the dream of making Grand Rapids a Top Five medical device manufacturing hub. We don't have enough engineers. We have plenty of engineering schools in Grand Rapids, Kalamazoo and to the east in the Detroit area.

But even if you start baking them today, it is going to be another four years before new engineers pop out of the university ovens.

So we are worried about not having enough new, young talent and we are worried about not having the venture capital or angel money that we would like to have.

This is not going to be a slam dunk.

Isn't this a great learning curve? Here we have yet another lesson the Medical Mile is teaching us that has to be transferred forward.

We have to do a better job of growing this generation of engineers and technicians needed to push manufacturing forward. We have really hurt ourselves by convincing our children the last place they want to land is in a factory.

What if Beery's dream is not realized?

Let's say for the sake of argument that the WMMDC falls short of its Top Five goal. How bad is that? Not so bad, according to Beery.

"The great thing with big, hairy audacious goals," he said holding his hand above his head, "is even if you miss it by a little you are still way higher than when you started."

Beery's attitude and the work of people like Rich Cook are duplicated about an hour south of Grand Rapids in Kalamazoo, where new businesses are being born on four feet of lab bench space in the Southwest Michigan Innovation Center.

Chapter Sixteen:
Four Feet of Bench Space

Dr. William E. Upjohn opened a small pill-producing business in Kalamazoo in 1866, a move that spawned one of the world's largest pharmaceutical players and would ultimately help shape the culture of that West Michigan city, about an hour south of Grand Rapids, in the 20th and 21st centuries.

Still, it was paper-manufacturing that moved Kalamazoo in the first third of the 20th century. The city and the small towns around it were home to 13 paper mills making 2.5 million pounds of paper every day.

Kalamazoo, like Grand Rapids, was powered by water. But, it wasn't the furniture industry that gave Kalamazoo its place in the world. It was the paper industry that put food on the tables of tens of thousands of people.

Just as Grand Rapids has its Grand River, Kalamazoo has a river bearing its name. However, Kalamazoo had a huge advantage over Grand Rapids. It is exactly halfway, a straight shot, between Detroit and Chicago. Kalamazoo has always been "connected."

Just as Grand Rapids had its furniture industry pioneers Kalamazoo had the people who brought the paper-making industry to town.

The paper mills were only one of the big guns that Kalamazoo had in its arsenal. It had auto manufacturing. Kalamazoo boosted a million-square-foot General Motors plant and miles of tool and die shops along with other industry suppliers to support it. The synergy was a wonderful thing to behold.

Kalamazoo also had science. The pharmaceutical industry was part of the economic stool upon which the city rested. Kalamazoo also had education. Western Michigan University was the top educational institution for decades on this side of the state. In fact, for a time, it was the only university.

The paper industry was to Kalamazoo what the auto industry was to Detroit and the furniture industry was to Grand Rapids. They built the cultures of their communities. Everyone knew the drill: Get out of high school with or without a diploma, get a job in the mills, or the factories, and you had a ticket to a middle-class lifestyle.

It all came crashing down, except Western Michigan University. Kalamazoo's place in the West Michigan higher education community was destined to grow.

But the other three legs of the stool broke one after another. Kalamazoo didn't only lose Big Paper; Kalamazoo also lost its place in the auto supply chain. And Kalamazoo lost Big Pharma. Upjohn, which was taken over by Pharmacia, which was taken over by Pfizer, closed facility after facility in Kalamazoo, Ann Arbor and Holland.

Kalamazoo made the same mistake as Detroit and Grand Rapids; they took it all for granted, until it was all gone. Consider that one of the critical takeaways from this page. No matter how good things are going today, we have to keep working on tomorrow's cluster of prosperity.

You can still see the collateral damage in Kalamazoo, just like in Detroit and Grand Rapids. People who worked in the paper mills, the pharmaceutical labs, the auto factories and the furniture plants are walking the streets, sitting on porches, toiling at Subway or laying on their couches. These are people who still seem shell-shocked, people who worked every day, worked hard and were proud of it, piling up the cash that came from all the hours of double-and-triple time, overtime, buying the toys, the lakeshore cottages. They are at home now wondering where it all went.

Kalamazoo chose a reinvention path similar to that taken by Grand Rapids. Just as Medical Mile was created on Michigan Street in Grand Rapids, the Business Technology and Research Park was born on the campus of Western Michigan University in Kalamazoo. Inside the BTR Park was built the Southwest Michigan Innovation Center (SWMIC), an incubator where four feet of lab bench space could give birth to the next great idea.

Western Michigan University is also building its own medical school. Kalamazoo shows a lot about its character in the way this institution is being put together. Benefactor names don't usually go on buildings in this city. You've heard of the Kalamazoo Promise? That is the guarantee that high school students will be able to go to college in Michigan without paying tuition. The people paying that bill chose to remain anonymous. In that spirit, WMU has received a $100 million gift to support the new school. The donors who signed one of the ten biggest checks ever written to a U.S. public university also wish to remain anonymous.

The new WMU medical school, slated to seat its first class in August 2014, is also an example of how the private sector has to be a part of reshaping a community, especially when the goal is this kind of change. MPI Research is donating a 330,000-square-foot building to WMU that will be used as the home of this new medical school.

Fans of historic irony will love this: "Building 267" as it is widely known in Kalamazoo, is a downtown science and research facility that once was part of the Upjohn, Pharmacia and Pfizer downtown campuses.

This new school also puts WMU into direct competition with the MSU College of Human Medicine in Grand Rapids for the federal and state grants that go to educational institutions of that kind and of course, faculty, researchers and students.

At the same time some of the companies inside the SWMIC serve customers based on Michigan Street in Grand Rapids. So, here is the question. Is this partnership, collaboration, competition, or all of the above?

Is SWMIC to be part of Medical Mile?

"That is a little bit of a political land mine," SWMIC CEO Rob DeWit admitted. "We have tremendous expertise. I wish we were better coordinated."

Is this partnership, collaboration, or competition? The correct answer is, "all of the above."

In Grand Rapids, the discussion is about "life sciences." In Kalamazoo, the discussion is about "health sciences." Southwest Michigan First CEO Ron Kitchens is very clear about why that difference is important.

Kitchens feels "health sciences" is "inclusive of the human condition." It is also a nice economic development umbrella that covers pharmaceuticals, medical devices, food and nutraceuticals, food safety, and the human condition of the hospital and the medical practitioner.

Here is one way that he and his counterpart in Grand Rapids, Birgit Klohs, are alike. Neither believes that life or health sciences is the silver-bullet cliché that will remake, remodel, reinvent or rebirth their communities.

However, they both see a need to grow these clusters of prosperity, these pods of innovation, if their regions are to prosper.

Southwest Michigan Innovation Center, this incubator of the future, the centerpiece of the Western Michigan University Business and Technology

Research Park is part of Ron Kitchens' strategy because, "you have to have the correct space for people."

Eighteen "client companies" were in that "correct space" at the time this book was written, with 133 employees, and annual payrolls totaling more than $7.5 million

Many of these companies are being led by displaced scientists, victims of the Big Pharma meltdown. They are learning to work without the security of a support system net under them that had been provided by Upjohn-Pharmacia-Pfizer. They are starting with just four feet of bench space in the Southwest Michigan Innovation Center incubator lab.

About half of the companies that have launched in the Innovation Center need wet labs. The Innovation Center provides that space. "They also provide a collegiality," said Ron. "So it is really kind of a group leadership of how to build a company, grow that company, a gathering point and a flagship point for companies."

Rich West did it on the four feet of bench space that was marked out for him at SWMIC. However, as Ron said, Rich and the others being incubated receive a lot more than just that. He also found the new environment that Kitchens described, an environment that was not all that different from where he came, Van Andel Institute.

This member of the new class of West Michigan entrepreneurs, born in 1971, is from a small town north of Traverse City, the true Northern Michigan, a land where skiing is so popular there are high school teams in that sport and when I lived up there you could rent cross-country skis from almost every gas station.

T-shirt, baseball hat on backwards, sunglasses and jeans. It is the uniform of Rich West the scientist, who also plays guitar, and is the husband of one and father of two. He lives in the small town of Coopersville more than an hour away from his four feet of bench space.

To follow Rich's professional journey is also to follow the evolution of the Grand Rapids health care community and the creation of the Medical Mile. He was working at Ferguson Hospital's department of pathology, doing clinical flow cytometry in Grand Rapids when that institution merged with Blodgett Memorial Medical Center. After Blodgett merged with Butterworth, Rich found himself working for Spectrum Health on the pediatric blood marrow transplant team, setting up and running the stem cell engineering program.

A Van Andel Research Institute investigator approached Rich in 2006 with a good job offer and one more line was added to his resume.

This is a big part of what makes Medical Mile so special. There are enough institutions on this mile-long, $1.5 billion campus to allow people like Rich West to grow and prosper without moving their families. It is also another lesson learned that has to be transferred forward: Talent needs a community with room for personal and professional growth.

Although he "loved it there (VARI), amazing people, amazing investigators and their mission, their vision, is really strong," Rich was off on his own four years later.

"I have an entrepreneurial gene that is highly expressed," he explained. "I wanted to do this forever and a day. I discussed it with my wife and she said, 'If this is what you really want to do, then maybe you should just do it.'"

He followed her advice and opened West Labs Scientific, LLC, conducting cellular analysis for biotech/pharma, research and academia all on four feet of bench space at Southwest Michigan Innovation Center in Kalamazoo.

Again, if you accept the definition of Medical Mile as inclusive of what is happening in Kalamazoo, this new community is large enough to allow talent like Rich West to grow and prosper. But he still has a small town —and Rich does love Coopersville – where he can raise a family.

Look easy? It is not.

Before you start on a journey similar to Rich's, you had better make sure that you have a plan in writing. Ron Kitchens and Southwest Michigan First don't have time for people who only dream. They want to talk to people who "do."

"We are not one of these groups that think you need a 400-page business plan," Ron assured me. "I would rather see three or four succinct pages that show me you have really thought out the problem and what your unique or novel solution is. What are the roadblocks? Who you are going to collaborate with? Who is the competition? How much capital it is going to take?"

If you aren't ready with that, or need assistance to put this plan together, SWMF will refer you to other groups that can help.

Let's assume you don't need that.

SWMF will send your three or four pages to a panel of experts for some "quick and dirty thoughts," with the expectation they will give it a thumbs up, or say, "this is an idea that has been tried 20 times before" and reject it.

If you are ready to move from "dream" to "do" here is an important word to remember.

GOOGLE

Never forget Google can be a noun or a verb. You have to know what Google is, as a noun, and how to use Google as a verb. Put your idea into Google and see what happens. Do it before you spend time writing up the three-or-four pages that Ron wants to see.

"It is amazing the number of times somebody comes in with a huge business plan, a tremendous investment in time and thought, and they never bother to Google (verb) it," he said. "We had someone come in the other day with an idea of how you could check your blood with an app on your cell phone. My team had just sat through a presentation from Sony on that."

Ron had to crush the poor guy's dreams, by showing him there were 30 versions of his great idea already available on Google (noun).

Assuming you get by all of that, and you have the IP to protect, SWMF moves you into a more intense due diligence phase, meeting with consultants who are on the economic development agency's payroll, to create some realistic growth milestones.

They might say the two words that entrepreneurs learn to dread: "Yeah, but…"

Here's the rub with health sciences. It is incredibly expensive to create a new drug or a new molecule. Advice to the entrepreneur: you are not going to be able to fund this yourself. That means the more successful your company becomes, the more likely it becomes that you are going to be fired.

If you can deal with that, you should also know that a new molecule from "start to pharmacist" is going to take 8-to-12 years. Who has that kind of time? It will cost between $1 billion and $3 billion so the exit strategy has to be selling it to Big Pharma.

If you don't get that, Ron isn't interested in you.

No problem. All you have to do is walk into Ron's office and tell him that your idea is going to make you rich in six months when you sell it to Big Pharma, and you will be more than happy to walk away.

That would also be a mistake.

Wait a minute. Isn't that what he told you that you had to understand? You don't get it.

You're right and you won't get it until you understand the "dual bottom line" that guides Southwest Michigan First.

There is a Triple Bottom Line (profit-environmental responsibility-social justice) that has been around for decades. There is a Quadruple Bottom Line (add in cultural responsibility) that has been around for years. But Ron and SWMF are driven by a Dual Bottom Line. And I think this is critical for all economic development in the 21st century. This is a most valuable, transferable lesson.

In a nutshell: you have to remember who brought you to the dance because "wealth" creation is just as important as "job" creation.

"We only want to invest in things that will bring wealth and jobs to the region," said Ron. "We will invest in things knowing that it is a product that will be sold to somebody. But if we are going to do that, it is going to have multiple impacts."

That means you are going to have to be contracting with local life science service providers, so that you are spending most of the money SWMF is going to get for you, locally. Otherwise it doesn't fit with their dual bottom-line strategy.

Of course the science has to make sense too. So if your idea meets all of the above criteria it is off to the SWMF Science Advisory board. That will take another 90 days while the science is re-verified.

SWMF is not going to be your sugar daddy. The agency never wants to hold more than 15-percent of the total investment in these early-stage projects, so they go out and sell it to angel investors, high-net worth individuals.

Here is a cold, hard fact about any venture capital investment and even though SWMF is a community interest-first kind of organization, Ron said, "This isn't a loan. We are buying majorities (i.e. control) of your company. If you are not willing to do that, don't take venture capital."

When everything is approved, the money is dispensed over a given time period when agreed upon milestones are met.

"Even then we get people who are not truly committed, who want their $5 million," said Ron. "It is a long process. It is a difficult process."

And, remember you have to go through all of those steps, give away part of your company, agree to move to Kalamazoo, grow jobs in Kalamazoo, and grow wealth in Kalamazoo. You have better learn to love Kalamazoo.

SWMF as befitting its community investment status is looking for total, and Ron means, total commitment.

However, that does not stop the idea flow. Ron said they see between 400 and 700 business plans a year and they never advertise. It is all word-of-mouth.

"I had 15 come in yesterday because I had done a webinar."

That is how it is today. However, Ron and his counterparts in Grand Rapids can see the need for a change. The due diligence will remain the same, but the opportunity for capital is about to expand.

Both communities, Kalamazoo and Grand Rapids are finding that just like the old models of economic development, and public-private sector partnerships needed to be re-tooled for the 21st century, so did the blueprints of finance. The way money changes hands will never be the same. At the very least, that is another dream.

CHAPTER SEVENTEEN:
A New Money Model

DIRK VLUG WAS A war hero when he arrived home in 1945. The Grand Rapid native destroyed five enemy tanks while serving in the Philippines and less than a year later would be awarded the Congressional Medal of Honor by President Harry Truman.

But like the millions of service men and women who were also coming home in the mid-1940s from World War Two and like the hundreds of thousands arriving back in the U.S. from Iraq and Afghanistan today, Dirk had no idea where he would find a job.

He and thousands of other veterans formed long lines outside a small counseling center in downtown Grand Rapids every day hoping to find work. [22]

It was not much easier to make a living before the war. Grand Rapids was coming out of the Great Depression when Dirk was drafted in 1940, just as the city was coming out of the Great Recession as the Medical Mile was beginning to blossom.

So, the effort to grow Medical Mile was not the first time that the Grand Rapids business and civic communities decided the city's economic base needed to be diversified nor was it the first time that the phrase "venture capital" was spoken in Grand Rapids.

A new money model was created coming out of the Great Depression, as city leaders found they could no longer rely on the decimated furniture industry. Fewer than half of the Grand Rapids companies that were producing furniture before the Depression years survived to the mid-1930s.

---

22   Gordon L. Olson, *Grand Rapids: A City Renewed*, (Grand Rapids: Grand Rapids Historical Commission, 1996), 1-3

The Grand Rapids Chamber of Commerce created Grand Rapids Industrial Corp. (GRIC) in 1935. It was a venture capital stock corporation. Armed with a bankroll of $125,000, GRIC issued more than 100 loans in 15 years to entrepreneurs who like their descendants on the Medical Mile needed financial backing.

Not all of the ideas flourished. However there was only one loan default by 1980 when GRIC was dissolved. It was a model that worked. The companies created with the help of its VC fund generated tens of thousands of jobs.

There is a history of Grand Rapids money backing Grand Rapids development. That legacy continued into the latter years of the 20th century when it was decided that the city's downtown was in need of a reinvention. Grand Valley State University President Emeritus Arend D. (Don) Lubbers told me he saw there was a problem when he and his wife moved to Grand Rapids in the late 1960s.

The city's business and civic leaders mobilized to commission Alexander Calder to create the "La Grande Vitesse" sculpture that would become a downtown landmark and the symbol of Grand Rapids.

"Diverse people came together to make things happen in Grand Rapids," Lubbers said. "So there was a 'make happen' system going."

Part of that system was a public-private sector partnership that brought the "Calder," as it is known, to Grand Rapids. There was private money raised, but National Endowment for the Arts funding capped off the drive. The sculpture was the first public work of art to be paid for with federal money.

Lubbers said that is when he began to see this group that had access to wealth beginning to take a leadership role in Grand Rapids.

Former Old Kent Bank President Dick Gillette, who Lubbers credits with leading the drive to get the Calder sculpture downtown, "brought Rich DeVos and Jay Van Andel in when they were starting to make big money, so the structure of getting people together and having citizen leadership participation to develop the community was there and that has continued to this day."

That is the model for how things get done in Grand Rapids.

As noted by the authors of a Metropolitan Policy Report at Brookings, "The substantial private investment in downtown amenities was a de facto major policy. The owners of Amway Corp. and Steelcase, along with their descendants, each poured hundreds of millions of dollars into the city and the region through individual and foundation gifts." [23]

It was an organized affair that would continue. The Grand Action Committee was formed and led the drive, using this public-private sector partnership model, to create a new convention center, DeVos Place and the city's new entertainment mecca, Van Andel Arena.

But would this public-private partnership model be enough to fuel Medical Mile? It was true that the second generation of the richest families in Grand Rapids were staying. It was also true that a second tier of money —not just billionaires, but millionaires—was marching in lock step with the DeVos and Van Andel drummers. The model was not broken. Could it be improved or reinvented?

The answer is "yes." A new financial model has emerged on the Medical Mile. And, just as life sciences would transform the business community, this new money model would shake the financial community to its core.

Outside money was coming to Grand Rapids. That is not the way they did it in 1935. It was not the way they did it in 1995 or 2005, either, aside from public sector funding.

"When you raise money in Grand Rapids, the first question is, 'who else is in?'" explained Dale Grogan, a partner at Charter Group in downtown Grand Rapids, and the managing director of Michigan Accelerator Fund 1, LP. "Then when they get that name, they call that person, talk to him and get back to you to say, 'I am in.'"

That is how it has always worked in Grand Rapids that is how it will always work. "And there is nothing wrong with that. But our mission here is to expand that 'old boys' network," said Grogan

While outside money is what got Silicon Valley started, that did not happen on Medical Mile. The historic approach in this conservative, parochial, West Michigan city has always been "those who have are those who give, and if they don't have enough, the project can wait."

"West Michigan has been very provincial in its approach to fundraising. We don't want to take in other partners because we don't know who these people are," Grogan told me. "That is a cloistered way of thinking and certainly is not conducive to venture capital."

That is changing, however, "as the community has matured...those shackles have come off."

---

23   Responding to Manufacturing Job Loss – June 2011 Metropolitan Policy Program at Brookings

This new financial model is also a shift from one of philanthropic giving, to one of pure investing; money making money.

Historically, the people who did give in Grand Rapids never expected a real return and did not see it as an investment beyond the tax breaks or the name on a building that might be the result. Okay. That is a little naïve. There was money to be made off the philanthropy if the giver owned the land on which a new public institution would be built or controlled the construction, etc. That still wasn't the same as just making money with money, a concept that almost seemed dirty or at least unseemly to the old money in Grand Rapids.

"But now it is turning towards investment," said Grogan. "That is really where the tipping point is, I think."

He pointed to the commercialization of research coming out of the Medical Mile as evidence of that move from philanthropy into investment, along with the impact on the business community of the MSU College of Human Medicine.

"The Medical Mile was rooted in philanthropy but it will flourish based on business," he stressed. "That is the critical take-home message."

Grogan sees this as the "dawning of a whole new age (in West Michigan) where you can unabashedly say, 'I made money as an investor and I am successful in doing that. That phenomenon is what made Silicon Valley what it is. You had smart people who made money in technology first, and then they took that money and invested it. They made more money, and made more money and that attracted more money."

Now it is time for the next stage in that evolution; the creation of true Medical Mile millionaires.

"It is the Google phenomenon," Grogan explained. "More than 140 millionaires came out of Google. They stayed in the Silicon Valley and became angel investors. That is what we have to create here."

Grogan said the Medical Mile will only thrive if it follows "the venture cycle."

1. Spawn good businesses
2. Invest in good businesses
3. Harvest good businesses and
4. Re-invest in other good businesses

"When you have done that," said Grogan, "one investment creates 10 millionaires, which creates 100 businesses, which creates 1,000 millionaires and so on. That is what has to occur here."

Grogan can see that happening on the Medical Mile. In fact, he is seeing it happen right now through the Michigan Accelerator Fund, which Charter Group manages out of their corporate office in downtown Grand Rapids.

They did their first deal five years ago with 12 investors and raised "a couple million dollars." Since then, progress has been made. The new model is being adapted. The community has matured in its investing sophistication enough that their most recent deal at the time of this interview was Grand River Aseptic Manufacturing.

That included 77 investors. They went up six-fold in the number of people who were willing to make capital risks, investment risks into their community." If this turns out as we hope, you will have 77 people who will say, 'hey, this works. Investment is fun,'" explained Grogan. "Then the next time you have 100 and then 200."

Still, there is what Grogan described as "an investment gap." Think about it this way. There are a handful of people who see every deal because they have enough money to put their names on the sides of buildings. Those are the people who can write the $1 million checks. The secret, he said, is to find the next level of investor who can write a check for $25,000.

"We are absolutely convinced that there are 1,000 guys in Grand Rapids who can write those $25,000 checks. They want to be in, but they don't have visibility, so they don't have deal flow."

This is about sustainability. A way to include that $25,000 investor has to be invented. There has to be some way to get a consistent deal flow to that person.

And, that is the secret discovered in Silicon Valley that needs to happen on the Medical Mile, according to Grogan.

"If you have good businesses, good entrepreneurs and good investors you have a sustainable financial eco-system," he said.

Ron Kitchens faces the same problem in Kalamazoo. It is the challenge shared by everyone in the West Michigan health and life sciences community.

Everyone knows the money inbred in Grand Rapids and Kalamazoo is a finite commodity. There is general agreement that it is going to take outside capital to grow dreams into ideas, then into deals, then into jobs and finally into community wealth.

Grand Rapids and Kalamazoo need new idea and revenue streams on the scale of the Grand and Kalamazoo rivers. Here is another lesson being taught by the Medical Mile. The people who live in those cities may think their hometowns are the best places on Earth, but the reality is, they are not the only places on Earth. And right now in this arena, they just don't stack up well.

As Ron explained, "When you are in San Jose, Boston, Houston or Austin, you don't have to leave your office. The deals flow to the venture capitalists in a never ending stream. "

Venture capitalists need to see deals to survive, given a best case scenario of getting it right on one in ten deals. Hopefully that one pays for the nine that don't make it. The return on investment is 25-to-35-percent.

The angel investor also needs deals. He or she is someone who wants to make a bunch of small bets or investments. Typically they do that based on nothing more scientific and analytic than gut instinct and the ability to read the guy across the table.

So in the end it is all about ideas and deals. You have to have an incredible volume to compete in this space. Right now, West Michigan is not in that league. But, Ron believes that by employing the right strategies, Grand Rapids and Kalamazoo will be able to compete.

"We have to show them that there are opportunities here that are lower cost and lower risk," Kitchens explained. "A traditional venture fund has one goal. That is to get as much return on investment as possible, in the shortest time possible."

"Venture capitalists are cowards," said Grogan. "All we want to do is to mitigate risk. We also want to, as engaged investors, bring checks or generate checks. More importantly, we want to generate business."

It is all about the ease of doing business and the size and speed of ROI. Closer to the office is always better; after all they are buying majorities of the companies in which they invest just like SWMF does.

This is a big problem for communities the size, scope and scale of Grand Rapids and Kalamazoo. How are we ever going to convince the VC funds in places like Boston and Austin to come to West Michigan?

Maybe we don't.

"We focus a lot of our attention on the Midwest because there isn't the arrogance or ignorance, depending on your perspective, of the big east and west coast VCs," Ron said. "But we also understand that we have to show our costs are significantly lower, the speed is significantly faster and the risk is minimized because of the quality of suppliers within the region."

SWMF is growing a long list of success stories to make that case. "Klaxon and MPI have taken niche markets, brought costs down and have been able to service customers all over the world from this region," said Ron.

"When we get a VC to visit they realize the quality, the people and the credentials are here, and say, 'that is the kind of investment that I want to make.'"

Of course there is nothing wrong with home cooking. Kalamazoo has plenty of millionaires and a couple of billionaires just like Grand Rapids.

SWMF has raised $65 million in last six years from people who have made their fortunes in Kalamazoo, want to reinvest in the community and help to grow jobs and to help create the next generation of wealth.

On the angel investor side of the private sector scale, Ron said they put together 11 deals, worth about $12.5 million. The smallest of those investors wrote a check for $50,000.

Next, he wants to open investment doors for everyone in Kalamazoo in areas other than what we are seeing on the Medical Mile and in the BTR Park. While life or health sciences product development is incredibly expensive, most other businesses do not require that kind of investment flow. The Kauffman Foundation has done a study showing the average business in America only needs about $25,000 in outside funding to stay viable.

And, as Ron told me, "not everyone wants to go to work in a white lab coat."

SWMF was planning to launch a new program in 2012 that is focused crowdfunding. The typical deal would be under $100,000 and people could get in for as little as $250 each. This could bring in new money from people the entrepreneur knows or maybe someone who just likes what they are doing.

The reinvention of the financial model in West Michigan is still evolving. . Third-generation philanthropist and visionary Rick DeVos started a "5x5" entrepreneur competition with a $5,000 grand prize. After only a couple of months, it became apparent that $5,000 was not enough. So, DeVos announced in late April 2012 that his family was launching the Smart Garden initiative, a $15 million venture capital fund that would be invested into literally hundreds of ideas every year.

Not every community has a DeVos family, or a Van Andel family or a Secchia family. Grand Rapids is extremely fortunate to have so many families who so much money who remain so committed to this American community.

However even if your community doesn't have a family of that financial magnitude lighting the entrepreneurial hallways, crowdfunding and the legislation signed by President Barack Obama to make that form of investment possible has opened new doors of financial freedom for those of us with ideas.

Ideas and money are only two important parts of the equation for community re-invention success. It has to be done with a plan.

"When we are bringing talent and capital around an idea, we want to be very strategic about it so that it is not just the horse, or the jockey, or the race track, or the entry fee to get the horse in the race," said Kitchens. "You have to do all four of those well. If you just do one, you still don't get to run in the race."

CHAPTER EIGHTEEN:
Leadership Needed

THE LACK OF VENTURE capital and angel investing is a problem on the Medical Mile. However, there is another challenge to deal with that could be much more difficult to overcome.

The Medical Mile is in desperate need of leaders. That is not to say there is crisis of leadership in the institutions on the Mile. The problem is there are not enough qualified people to run the next generation of businesses that are on the Michigan Street NE launch pad.

It is hard to believe that is a problem in a city like Grand Rapids with such a strong history of business leaders, visionaries and CEOs. They created and then led companies like Steelcase, a Grand Rapids-based business that began by hammering wastebaskets out of steel. The generations that followed created iconic office furniture systems for the world.

It was Peter M. Wege Sr. who came up with the idea of making furniture out of metal and then convinced Walter Idema and 10 other men to form the Metal Office Furniture Company in 1912.

Wege put the title "president" on his office door in 1914, the same year that Metal Office received its first patent for the Victor fireproof steel wastebasket. That was a simple invention necessitated by a real problem. Office buildings were burning down because men were flicking their hot cigar ashes into wooden wastebaskets filled with paper.

Grand Rapids' business history books are filled with men like Peter Wege who built solid companies from relatively small ideas. It was the generations that followed him that guided Steelcase for 100 years, through the boom years following World War Two, the depressing years when manufacturing was collapsing all around us in Michigan, and then through the reinvention of the 21st century.

Stories like that are waiting to be told on Medical Mile.

Jerry Callahan is one of the managing directors of Hopen Life Sciences Ventures, a fund that reached a $25 million initial close for its second fund in August 2011, with a target of $50 million that was expected to be reached by January 2012. He is also vice president of business development for the Van Andel Research Institute and interim CEO of Intervention Insights.

He identified the lack of leadership as a far more dangerous problem for the Mile than the lack of money, during a conversation in his office in the Van Andel Research Institute. Jerry told me that Medical Mile needs people who know how to drive the new businesses that we hope to see created on Michigan Street NE.

Callahan knows how to grow things. But Jerry can't do it all himself. He has more than 15 years of operational leadership experience and serves on the board of several private equity and venture capital organizations focused on the life sciences. Jerry has a Ph.D. in organizational leadership and his primary job at VARI is to grow businesses that are spun out of research.

"Our goal is to prove the principle, get the thing (company) started, show some momentum and then sell it," he said. "We are really leveraging all of the assets that Michigan has to offer."

The development and roll out of Intervention Insights, a Van Andel Institute spin-out, is a demonstration of what he does and the biggest challenge facing Medical Mile.

Intervention Insights is a company that wants to change the way the world fights cancer by using the human genome and cancer patients' genes to create a personalized strategy for battling the disease.

The company's website claims that by analyzing cancerous tissue, "we can generate a genomic picture of over 20,000 genes and corresponding molecular pathways that uniquely define a person's cancer and the drugs that target them. We deliver this information to our frontline oncology partners who can quickly review hundreds of drugs which specifically target the molecular basis of a person's cancer."

At the time he invited me into his office, Callahan, who speaks faster than most other humans on this planet, was serving as launch CEO of Intervention Insights, while a national search for a permanent replacement was being conducted.

Common wisdom is that a lack of money -- venture capital and angel investment-- is the biggest problem facing the quest to spin out quality life sciences companies on Medical Mile. Callahan disagrees.

"Money is obviously the necessary fuel for a bio-tech, life-sciences or any start-up business," he asserted. "Access to adequate funding is certainly critical. There is no doubt about that. But I would put that as number-two on our priority list of what we are lacking in West Michigan."

He believes what Medical Mile needs more than money is a stable of accomplished CEOs and executive talent to lead the bio tech and life science companies that we hope will be generated by the Mile's research, just like the company former VARI researcher Rich West is pushing forward in Kalamazoo.

Running a start-up is something you can't do, until you have done it. The Mile is in desperate need of experienced people who have done it time and time again. "I can always find money for a good idea. Once people know we are here and we have money, ideas come to us," said Callahan. "But can I get the leadership team that we need to actually run the company? That is the challenge we have had so far."

There are people who do this on the East and West coasts. And they are good at it. That is not to say these people get it right every time. They don't. This is not easy. The failure rate is incredibly high. That is why we need so many more start-ups on the Mile to attract the people who can drive them.

"Let's say our scientists find one molecular mechanism, or a gene that seems to be really important in treating colorectal cancer. From that first discovery, if I have 10,000 guys who come to me and say, 'Hey, I found a molecular mechanism that seems to control this disease,' I get one drug out the other end. It is a 10,000 to 1 failure rate."

The good news is that with every small victory the chances of ultimate success improve. Once they uncover an entity, a drug, a food or a device that can affect that disease they are down to a 1,000 to 1 failure rate.

Once they prove that it works in an animal system and it is safe, remember Clorox is probably the world's best cancer-fighting agent, but the side effects would be brutal, the failure rate is something like 100 to 1. That is when investors start getting involved and a launch CEO would take over.

The failure rate of a medical device is better, but it is still pretty high. A grim fact of life all launch CEOs have to deal with is that no matter how good he or she is the drug or device could still bomb out.

"If I have a professional batting average of .300, it puts me in the top ten percent of Major League Baseball. It also puts me at the top of all CEOs," Callahan explained. "But it also means out of every 10 jobs I take, I am going to fail seven times."

So, that launch CEO has to live with the knowledge that chances are he or she will be out of work in a matter of a year to three years, living off a severance package if they were lucky enough to get one, looking for their next opportunity.

That is acceptable in a place like Boston where there is a much higher number of life sciences, bio tech and medical device companies being launched. The professional launch CEO can always find a similar position in that city. "He should have another job in 60 days to six months if he's had a track record of a 30 percent success rate," Jerry explained. "That is not going to happen in Grand Rapids. He knows if he fails he is probably going to have to leave the city."

Medical Mile is not only dealing with a problem of quantity. It is facing a challenge of what could be called, "perceived quality." Think of it as a problem of reputation. Grand Rapids is not seen as the most attractive place in the world to work. It is seen by many, if they can even find it on the map, as just another Midwestern city that is awfully long on winter, short on flavor and very vanilla.

However, Callahan said he had seen some blogs lately that are describing West Michigan in general and Grand Rapids in particular in a much more favorable light.

"There is a significant groundswell of new information on the blogs that say West Michigan is a place to go for innovation and entrepreneurship in life sciences," he said. "But we need to do more of that."

That is a very positive development for Callahan who has had to go outside of West Michigan to find the leadership teams he needed for the four companies that have been spun out of Van Andel Research Institute.

"I had to bring people in from Indiana to run one company, a San Francisco team to run another company and a team from San Diego bought the other company," he said.

So, bringing this caliber of CEO to Grand Rapids is tough, but not impossible. After all he did find CEOs that were willing to come to Grand Rapids. What was the carrot that attracted those people? And what was the deal maker that convinced them to stay?

"We had to prove the principle," he said. "We invested high-risk capital early on to show that not only did we think it was a good idea, we proved it was a good idea. We 'de-risked' it for them."

That is not best case, or worst case. It is the only case. It is the only model to follow until the kind of volume develops on Medical Mile and in West Michigan that is needed to create a cluster or community of local launch CEOs who can engage with these early-stage companies.

"When you start anything new, you have to buy your way into the market," said Callahan. "The blessing that we have is that we had a significant part of the clinical and research market already bought for us, a little over $3.5 billion."

That is the head start that the creation of Van Andel Institute and Spectrum Health, along with the investments made by Grand Valley State University and Michigan State University delivered for the West Michigan life sciences, bio tech and medical device communities.

"The good news is we placed a $3.5 billion bet," said Callahan. "The bad news is we placed a $3.5 billion bet. We have to leverage that money."

Dave Van Andel knows all about that bet. His father Jay is responsible for $1 billion of it, money donated to open Van Andel Institute.

Dave also understands what it is like to do business in Grand Rapids and to convince people to not take care, as their mothers might caution, but to take a risk.

"Grand Rapids is a dichotomy in that respect. Our conservative roots don't lend well to a high degree of risk taking. Ironically there are a large number of entrepreneurs that come out of West Michigan. I don't know why that is," he laughed, "but they do and you don't have to look very far. The names on the buildings will tell you who they were. And yet the culture is almost counter-intuitive to that."

Van Andel feels there is a "great work ethic" and other "value streams" in the West Michigan culture. "But we have not built the infrastructure in our banking systems or in our support in the community for those risk takers to want to be resident here."

The business history books are filled with the names of people who have helped build Grand Rapids and West Michigan. Steelcase, Herman Miller, Gentex, and more were all built by visionaries who took a risk and were able to convince others to back them.

But there was also the story of William P. Lear, a visionary born in Missouri who wound up in Grand Rapids, inventing the F-5 automatic pilot for jet aircraft and the first eight-track tape that could be played in cars.

He left Grand Rapids when the board of his corporation rejected the idea of building an affordable executive jet airplane. Lear didn't blink. He sold $10 million worth of stock and moved to Wichita, Kansas where he created that jet for business executives, and founded Lear-Siegler.

Risk aversion like that could cripple the Medical Mile. However, the Lear's board of trustees had a fiduciary responsibility that they were sworn to uphold. They must have realized that not every great idea is really all that great. How many times did Thomas discover ways that a light bulb would not work? Most great ideas are bound to fail. Lear was a millionaire at the age of 29, but lost it all betting on the creation of a steam-powered automobile.

Grand Rapids needs to come to grips with that, not just for life sciences but in general, because it is vitally important to have a constant flow of entrepreneurs, if you want to generate economic vitality. West Michigan inventors do get a lot of patents, but we don't have enough talent here to take those ideas to market.

Remember how Grand Rapids lost the production of Lear Jet. It was by being too conservative, too unwilling to take a risk.

Southwest Michigan Innovation Center CEO Rob DeWit is also worried about the lack of launch CEOs even though that was supposed to be one of Kalamazoo's strongest suits. The implosion of Upjohn/Pharmacia/Pfizer left the city with hundreds of trained scientists looking for labs. It also left Kalamazoo with hundreds of big Pharma executives looking for new C-level suites they could continue shepherding the lab coats into a profitable 21st century.

So far, it is not working out that way. Or if it has, it is certainly on a much smaller scale than the dream that was sold in the first years of West Michigan's re-build.

"I hear that. I think we have lost some of our C-level leadership in the last decade or so, but I don't think that has to be permanent," DeWit told me.

"We never have had any difficult in recruiting to Kalamazoo. If the energy stays high, that will come back. Michigan is a great place to live. When people understood that they didn't want to leave. There are a lot of people who would like to come back."

We have to circle back to the money. It is always the money, isn't it? Dave Van Andel pointed out that once Medical Mile has that stable of CEOs to guide the start-ups, Grand Rapids will need to have the banking and investment infrastructure in place so that these companies can create, develop and move products to market.

"This is the last step in the process we have been putting together," said Van Andel. "And, it is the hardest part because there is a lot that is unproven there."

This is another new concept for a lot of people inside and outside the Mile. Ideas don't have to be born here to be good ideas. This runs counter to the Grand Rapids culture. Take a long look through the city's business history. After the original influx of entrepreneurs, most of the successful men were born and bred here.

Callahan believes it is true that just as money will follow ideas and ideas will follow money, ideas know no borders. "We do not have a corner on the market for good ideas. No one does. Most of the ideas in the Silicon Valley don't come from the Bay area; they are born into the Bay area and grow in that fertile ground. We need to create that kind of fertile ground here."

Even though Grand Rapids has a history of being very parochial, Callahan said there is no rule on Medical Mile that says all ideas have to be home-grown. Quite the contrary, Callahan also knows there are no borders when it comes to finding the next great idea or better said the next great experiment.

"If we can prove we are a good bed of economic activity and entrepreneurship with proven leaders, ideas will come here," he said. "People with dot-com ideas go to Silicon Valley. They don't question that. We need to have the same kind of groundswell to attract the same kind of critical mass. Once that happens, ideas will follow. I am not worried about that."

This all raises the question, "What does Grand Rapids really want Medical Mile to become?" It is a question that is still being debated while this American community is reinvented.

CHAPTER NINETEEN:
Medical Mile or Mecca?

MAYBE MEDICAL MILE WON'T work. Nothing in the world has a God-given right to be successful. The vision was that the Mile would create a new industry at a time when it was desperately needed, that Medical Mile would improve the quality of life in metro Grand Rapids by bringing a diversity of people into the region, and that the Medical Mile would also improve the quality and lower the cost of health care in the community.

Michigan Street NE, home to Medical Mile, is bustling with an extraordinary level of activity and new industry. Hearts are being transplanted on the Mile. Researchers are making progress in their quests to cure cancer, Parkinson's, Alzheimer's and other diseases that plague humanity.

Yet, Alliance for Health President Lodewyk (Lody) Zwarensteyn is not satisfied. He has been watching the Mile closer than anyone because Lody runs an organization that is all about keeping an eye on the health care community to make sure it operates in the interests of this American community.

He wants Medical Mile to become a Medical Mecca. Lody envisions a day when the Mile competes with the Mayo and Cleveland clinics for patients from around the world. He doesn't see that happening now. Beyond that, Zwarensteyn isn't sure that the people in the C-level suites care enough about the Grand Rapids community.

That is not to belittle what has happened on Michigan Street NE. Lody told me during a conversation in his office that he buys into the concept of Medical Mile being more than what we are seeing on Michigan Street, pointing out that "you cannot ignore Mary Free Bed Hospital and Saint Mary's (Health Services) that are downtown. And you can't ignore Michigan Blue Cross."

Saint Mary's Health Services, as we documented in an earlier chapter, has created its own version of Medical Mile and is working in close collaboration with Van Andel Institute, MSU and Spectrum Health. Saint Mary's, like Spectrum, is counting on a lot reinvestments by the organization's physicians.

No one has all the answers to everything. Perfection in health care, the mark of excellence, becoming one of the top 100 hospitals: does that come as a result of the staff in place now or the staff that will be there tomorrow? Perhaps more importantly: how does the cost of health care relate to the quality of health care?

Zwarensteyn didn't waste any time telling me that "the best health care is usually the least costly."

Lody was very concerned about the cost of health care in West Michigan when we met in his small office. Zwarensteyn has been a fixture in the development of the Medical Mile since the days of the Hillman Commission's recommendation that led to the Butterworth Hospital-Blodgett Medical Center merger. He remembers the promises that were made.

If the health care institutions on Medical Mile do not do a better job of containing costs, the price of health care can't fall in the Grand Rapids community and Zwarensteyn does not think Grand Rapids will ever see a Medical Mecca created.

"We want to be in the top one-percent of performance. But we also want to have the lowest price," said Zwarensteyn as he turned down the classical music playing on his stereo. "You can do that through coordination, through pencil sharpening, through some conservative attitudes in the community."

Zwarensteyn senses a new attitude on Medical Mile and in the Grand Rapids medical community, a philosophy that he doesn't like. There is a new cast of players on Michigan Street. Some of the old remain, but new blood is flowing. He said these new players are not working to lower the cost of health care.

An unintended consequence of the Old Guard leaving the Grand Rapids health care community could be a failure to collaborate and cooperate on Michigan Street. It could be that the shared vision that created the Mile has vanished. Maybe all of this new blood really isn't what we need. Or at the very least, he believes that the culture that created Medical Mile is not being transferred to the next generation. Zwarensteyn said there are stresses to that decades-old culture because outsiders with a different set of values, and a different mindset about the business of medicine, are moving in to the Medical Mile community.

"Some people feel they have to run their program like a business, responsible only to their program, measured only by their program's relative success," he explained. "That does strain the collaborative because it does stress 'we want to get ahead,' and that is 'we as opposed to you.' We do have some of those tensions."

"Some of our hospital administrators, quite candidly, need their hospital boards to sit on them and tell them to be collaborative."

Metro Health Executive Vice President Dr. William "Bill" C. Cunningham told me that he is also sensing a real problem with collaboration on Medical Mile. Bill sees relationships on the Mile as being more physician-to-physician these days, rather than C-suite relationships that used to dominate the local health care community. Cunningham makes life on the Mile sound kind of cold.

Why? Like Lody, Cunningham thinks it has a lot to do with medicine becoming a business, or perhaps better put; it has everything to do with that business of medicine being run with a competitive, corporate mentality.

"As it becomes more of a business it gets less personalized," Cunningham said. "So it is like two bankers who shake hands and smile at each other, but then they go back to their own offices and develop strategies to outthink each other."

Just as Lody told me, Bill said for years the hospitals had a close working relationship until the institutions created separate business models. Cunningham reminded me that there used to be a Grand Rapids Area Hospital Board that included hospital CEOs and some board members from each institution.

"The reason that fell apart was that they were all going to do a cancer center together, but several of the administrators didn't want to do that, they didn't want to share."

That spawned new competition, and although he obviously yearns for the way it was, Cunningham said the new blood that brought a new corporate culture to Medical Mile has not been all bad for West Michigan.

"The community-at-large has been the beneficiary of that. When you look at this area's health care prices and 'bang for your buck,' and compare that to what is going on in Kalamazoo just 40 miles to the south, you will find their prices are 20, 30 and even 40 percent higher."

He also said the West Michigan business community has gotten very involved in the delivery of health care, has kept prices low and has created

Medical Mile; something that Cunningham believes has to be considered a real bonus for the region.

"For example, I think it is fantastic and I applaud the people who gave the money for (Helen DeVos) Children's Hospital," he explained. "It means we don't have to go to Ann Arbor or Detroit to take care of our children or grandchildren."

Bill also believes health care resources are going to become scarcer and government money to help fund all of these systems will be reduced in the future "so, we need to work together," he explained. "We need to do more consolidation, even though I know that is a dirty word around here."

Cunningham would like to see the MSU colleges of Osteopathy (in the Metro Health Village) and Human Medicine (on the Medical Mile) come together like they did in the past. He thinks they should share resources in the first two years of medical school when MSU students, in the recent past, took a lot of the same courses together.

Will any of that happen? He chuckles, "I think there has to be some impetus from the people in the community to get the (health care) CEOs together and say that this is what has to happen. That has to be part of the hospital CEOs' initiatives."

Lody also warns of a competitive, corporate mindset in the West Michigan health care community. He thinks that concept is at odds with the very conservative and collaborative nature of metro Grand Rapids.

Lody said the community built itself over generations on values of thrift, cooperation, and non-waste and value service. "We want the right thing done at the right time for the right price. The community for generations has been intolerant of waste, public or private. That has been a core value of Grand Rapids," Zwarensteyn pointed out. "Taj Mahals, we don't build."

The merger of Butterworth and Blodgett brought together two of the best hospitals in the U.S. They were both Top 100 hospitals. It was a master stroke for the community. What happened to the senior management that shared the vision? They are gone. "The new management was imported and whether they have embodied the values of the community is subject to question," asserted Zwarensteyn.

Another problem that Lody pointed to was a lack of a coordinated marketing campaign, a marketing strategy, to tell the story of Medical Mile. He is bothered by all of the billboards, radio, TV and newspaper ads that each of the hospitals run in metro Grand Rapids. Lody maintains that is like preaching to the choir or maybe it is like preaching to your neighboring church's choir, trying to get them to sing with your congregation.

Medical Mile needs to bring in new business. Zwarensteyn made that point in our conversation. He believes a coordinated effort has to be made to "convince that doctor in Tupelo" to refer his or her patient here, instead to the Mayo Clinic or the Cleveland Clinic. That is not happening now, at least not to the degree that Zwarensteyn believes is necessary.

If Medical Mile only serves West Michigan, he pointed out it will only churn local dollars that would have been spent in the region anyway. "We would just be cannibalizing our area," Lody said.

Not everyone agrees. While bringing new patients, doctors and money into West Michigan would be a bonus, Spectrum Health CEO Rick Breon stressed in an earlier chapter that medical care is as local as politics, usually delivered within a 120-mile radius.

Still, Zwarensteyn said the West Michigan medical community, needs to come together with a comprehensive marketing strategy to answer one key question: What would give that doctor the idea and the incentive to refer a patient to Grand Rapids?

It is not easy to break a referral pattern. "It can be done. But it will take a new marketing strategy," he said.

However, there is a difference between selling dreams and changing reality. Zwarensteyn said the Medical Mile is going to have to offer doctors outside of West Michigan an advantage to refer his or her patient to Grand Rapids. That is not just quality of care. That is not just lower price. That is everything. It is all of the system, all of the institutions, all of everything working together on the Mile.

That is why collaboration and a unity of purpose and vision are so critical. That is what brought Medical Mile into being. Without it, Zwarensteyn said, Medical Mile will never realize its potential.

"What if Blue Cross was to say that 'you get a break if you come to Grand Rapids instead of Mayo' or what if the newspaper was to say 'come to Grand Rapids where you will get great care?'"

Just like Jerry Callahan, who believes Medical Mile needs to bring investors to West Michigan to see the real Grand Rapids, Zwarensteyn said that doctors have to be enticed to come to the city to see what is really happening on Medical Mile.

"All of those things build on each other."

Is that happening now? The answer is, "yes." Spectrum Health people do travel the nation, and so do people from Saint Mary's. MSU College of Human Medicine people do the same thing. They also invite doctors to Grand Rapids for symposia and meetings. The VAI's Dr. Craig Webb told us in an earlier chapter that he doesn't have to "sell" Grand Rapids as hard as he used to, but he still is "a voice at the podium," as Rick Breon put it.

But, is this a concerted effort? Zwarensteyn doesn't think so. He said if that was the case it would mean that all of the systems and institutions were working together. Is that happening?

"How supportive of Spectrum is Blue Cross going to be if Spectrum says 'as of this date we are no longer going to accept Blue Cross payment?' How supportive is Saint Mary's going to be of Spectrum if Spectrum says 'we don't want Saint Mary's to get into that service or this service or vice versa?'"

"How will physicians react if they are told that if they don't become employees of a particular institution they will not have privileges? Or what if a health plan tells doctors they will not be reimbursed the same as others unless they do whatever?"

He warns that all of those threats going on behind the scenes, as they are now, threaten to "vulcanize" a community against something with the potential of a Medical Mile.

"We can't have a vulcanized community," said Zwarensteyn. "We need a unified community. As long as the trustees are not firmly keeping the culture set in a collaborative direction, we will have a culture that has the stresses that will make sure we are not that Medical Mecca."

And who pays the bill for everything that is happening if patients don't come in from Tupelo? It could be said, as Zwarensteyn did, that West Michigan does not build "Taj Mahals." But Grand Rapids came close on the Medical Mile. Who is going to pay for that if health care spending is simply churned?

"There is a reckoning at some time for all of that," warned Zwarensteyn.

The promise was made that the community, at some time, would reap the benefits of the Butterworth-Blodgett merger that created Spectrum Health.

"And yet look at the cost increases in premiums and prices of services," said Zwarensteyn. "We are still in the lowest quartile and people are comfortable with that. But we could be so much lower if we wanted to. That is the problem."

He strongly disagrees with those who say medical prices have been dropping, pointing to West Michigan employers who are struggling to pay 40-45-percent premium increases. Most of their health care spending use is in this community. So where did that increase come from? How has the Medical Mile really helped them?

"It is not like all of a sudden we had 15 heart transplants all at one work place," said Zwarensteyn. "We just don't have that many heart transplants. (The prices) for a lot of services have escalated without shame."

Lody also said that Alliance for Health has consistently asked the hospital boards to review their charges and lower them. But they don't. If this continues, he argued, we will be killing the goose that laid the golden egg.

What has to happen to change this? He believes the Mile does need a leader with vision and a sense of purpose. But Medical Mile, Lody said, also needs a leader or a new class of leaders that won't be undercut by a CEO or a COO or a whole class of C-suite people which has a culture that says "we are going to run this like a business and the more profit we make the better."

The problem with some hospitals is that they are more concerned with shareholders than stakeholders.

"And we will have a very good system, but it will be an expensive system that many people will not be able to access financially," he said. "And you can carry that on until sometime, when if we get a single-payer system, the cost will be spread over the whole tax base and people will feel better. I don't know."

You can sense that Lody is not happy with the culture of the Medical Mile. There was a different feeling at Day One. He was there. "The spirit was much better then," said Zwarensteyn. "Oh, there were pressures. Somebody always wanted to be on first before the other guy. But you could always bring them down by asking 'what's best for the community?'"

"Right now we have some people who are saying, 'we are the community. We will decide what's best' that is dangerous."

Zwarensteyn said it is getting so that you can cut the hubris with a knife on Medical Mile.

"We have people who believe their own press releases right now. And we are getting people in hospital PR fired right now because they are not getting their hospital enough air time."

He believes that is so misdirected, not just because of the ego it takes to make that kind of a decision, but because of the misguided marketing that aims its message at the converted with a best-case result of churning West Michigan money.

Everyone is in bed together on the Mile, but everyone is still tugging the blanket this way and that way.

"If we put billboards all over this community what is that saying, who are we talking too? Why don't we put those billboards in Tupelo? Are we kidding ourselves?" Zwarensteyn said.

"We have a great future. The potential is tremendous. But we won't realize it until we see that patient coming in from Tupelo."

CHAPTER TWENTY:
Rattling the Cage

"'WE SCREWED UP': GRAND Rapids restaurant owners vow to be ready for ArtPrize crowds next weekend" The headline in *The Grand Rapids Press* said it all, Sept. 28, 2009. [24]

Nobody saw it coming, or better put, nobody saw them coming. Crowds estimated at 20,000 swarmed into downtown Grand Rapids for the first ArtPrize. Restaurants started running out of food Saturday night. Those that were able to open Sunday were swamped with the hungry and thirsty before they too ran out of food.

Grand Rapids never saw ArtPrize coming. This was Rick DeVos' idea. The grandson of Rich, the son of Dick –who had run for Governor and lost, is very soft-spoken and low-key. He was the first of the third generation to really take a step forward with an idea for an art festival, called ArtPrize. And we thought, "that has been done before. What could he be thinking of?"

This was not the first time Grand Rapids had celebrated art. Summer traditionally begins with the Grand Rapids Festival of the Arts, known to most of us as simply "Art Fest" or "Festival" but Seinfeld fans do refer to it as "Festivus." It takes over the downtown district for one weekend, but never comes close to DeVos' ArtPrize, an event that is growing more international every year. Festival of the Arts, on the other hand is much more local. It is like a backyard talent show for the city and its suburbs. It is always a money loser. But as former Mayor John Logie used to proclaim, "It is the largest all-volunteer festival of its kind in the U.S."

---

24   Chris Knape, "'We screwed up:' Grand Rapids restaurant owners vow to be ready for ArtPrize crowds next weekend" *M-Live.com The Grand Rapids Press*, Sept. 28, 2009. Accessed May 5, 2012.

It seems like everyone who is in a band gets on the stage during Festival of the Arts. All the community, school and private dance classes perform and every community service agency or church in the region sells food to raise money. Festival of the Arts is ingrained in the culture of Grand Rapids. However, it is always the same every year even down to the annual wind and/or rain storm that will knock down all of the tents on cue at least one afternoon of Festival weekend and send the crowds scurrying for cover.

So how big could this "ArtPrize" idea be? The most cynical among us just figured the DeVos family could do whatever it wanted to do in downtown Grand Rapids, and they were doing it.

Rick tried to warn us the best he could in a You Tube video, telling us that Art Prize 2009 would turn downtown Grand Rapids into an art gallery.

"This came out of going to a lot of events – Sundance, SXSW, TED – and seeing the power of those events and what the artists added to those communities," he said. The fact that he delivered this message on YouTube instead of going through the usual Grand Rapids media mule train should have given us a clue that this would really shake up our world. And it did.

"What could he be thinking?" we wondered. In his soft-spoken way, Rick was talking about inviting artists from around the world to come to downtown Grand Rapids for a non-juried, totally open art show with a $250,000 grand prize.

Looking back on it now, it made perfect sense. Just as the life sciences world was being invited to the Medical Mile, Rick DeVos was inviting the art world into Grand Rapids.

"This is all about experimentation and conversation," Rick said in that YouTube video. "We are changing the idea of what a gallery is. The city is the gallery."

We so didn't get it. We so underestimated the impact this would have, and after interviewing him for WOOD Radio, I think Rick was blown away by it, too. Tens of thousands of people came to downtown Grand Rapids for the first weekend of ArtPrize 2009. It was an incredible wake-up call for the community.

ArtPrize 2009 brought a new world to downtown Grand Rapids. Not only were there more people than we had ever seen on a Sunday, we were looking at art that we weren't sure was really art. We were pretty sure some of it was disturbing. As Rick warned in that introductory YouTube video, "There are no limits on format. This is all about creative expression and reaction to that expression." Amen to that.

The displays in the 2009 version of Art Prize included a mobile made from Sticky Notes, the sculpture of a moose made entirely from 60,000, 9-inch roofing nails (winning the fifth place prize), a replica of the Loch Ness monster floating in the Grand River, and a giant table-and-chairs sculpture perched on top of a bridge over that waterway. There were some truly unusual exhibits.

The artist, Ran Ortner, won the $250,000 prize for his painting, "Open Water." Second place went to the artist of an outdoor mural. One of the more unusual works of art took the third-place prize. Eric Daigh won $50,000 for "Portraits," three 4X6 foot portraits done entirely with stick pins. He used 50,000 stick pins for each portrait.

There was also 100,000 paper airplanes dropped on the 20,000 people on Monroe Center, all in the name of art, by a Grand Rapids Community College student, Rob Bliss. He had already made his name in Grand Rapids by using zombies to introduce the city to the power of social media.

Best estimates put the number of people in full zombie costume and make-up at better than 4,000 on the night of Oct. 30, 2008. Bliss used Facebook, totally bypassing the usual media connections, to try to break the Guinness world record for the number of zombies walking at one time.

What a night that was. It was total fun for everyone but the GRPD and a lot of people who hung on to their humanoid mentality. The police were already stretched thin with crowd control for a Van Andel Arena event. Now they had to worry about this: Zombies parading through downtown Grand Rapids, scaring people on the sidewalks, slithering over cars stopped at traffic lights. It was nuts. History was being made.

We all think Bliss did break the record. However, there was a problem with certification. That really doesn't matter. What does matter is that we learned the power of social media, a force that was completely new to most of Grand Rapids. That was an excellent lesson for the next cluster of prosperity and the expansion of Medical Mile: Social media can't be ignored. It needs to be used not only for communication, but also for collaboration. Another lesson: Never underestimate the next generation.

Bloody zombie clothing littered downtown streets the next morning. Police officials complained about the behavior of the zombies. What did Grand Rapids City Hall do? Mayor Heartwell and the rest knew a winner when they saw one. They brought Bliss into their fold and he began putting on city-sponsored events to break world records, like the one for the most people drawing with chalk on sidewalks or the biggest downtown water slide.

His best was yet to come. Bliss was able to mobilize 30,000 people for something that caught the world's attention, the "Grand Rapids Lip Dub." The whole city got into this. Thirty-thousand people, according to best estimates, spent a day downtown, doing a continuous lip synch to "American Pie," by Don McLean.

"We got so lucky," Bliss told The Grand Rapids Press May 23, 2011. "We created the world's largest and longest lip dub video in just four hours."[25]

The timing could not have been better. Grand Rapids was still reeling from a Newsweek magazine story that ranked the city as #10 on a list of America's Dying Cities.

Mayor Heartwell fired off a stinging response to Newsweek editor Tina Brown, beginning the city's defense by pointing to the Medical Mile. "Dear Ms. Brown: The citizens of Grand Rapids were astounded when you declared our city, Grand Rapids, to be a "dying city" in the January 21, 2011 issue of Newsweek.

Dying city? Surely Newsweek must be joking! Would a major medical school (Michigan State University School College of Human Medicine) move its campus to a dying city?"

Still the Newsweek article was out there. Grand Rapids needed a public relations shot in the arm to cure what was ailing it, both externally and internally.

The Grand Rapids Lip Dub was that, and more. It took YouTube and the Internet by viral storm and made Grand Rapids and the people who live here, whether they were in the video or not, stars for weeks. Toronto. com called it "the video that saved a city."

It was the same for ArtPrize. We got way more than 15 minutes of attention out of it.

Thanks to ArtPrize 2009, we discovered that Grand Rapids was the best kept secret from ourselves. It had much more to offer than most of us thought. It was then I realized, "I really can live in this city." First time I ever felt that way. This was finally not the city I moved into in 1990. It also showed us the attraction Grand Rapids could become. It was suddenly a destination city. ArtPrize also celebrated the community. And, remember how important that is when it comes time to attract more

---

25   Jeffrey Kaczmarczyk, "Rob Bliss releases trailer for Grand Rapids Lip Dub video of Don McLean's American Pie filmed Sunday, *M-Live Grand Rapids Press*, May 23, 2011. Accessed May 5, 2012.

talent to Medical Mile and the first wave of pioneers for our next cluster of prosperity.

ArtPrize was a big deal in 2009. It was a major event in 2010. However, we were totally blown away the following year. ArtPrize 2011 was huge. It was a 19-day event, running from September 21 through October 9. There were so many people in downtown Grand Rapids on the final weekend, you didn't have to walk. You just stood still and the crowd moved you. I absolutely did not believe it when I walked the mile-and-a-half from my home to downtown Grand Rapids.

The crowd of people making this pilgrimage like me just kept growing. First one family joined me on the sidewalk in the Heritage Hill neighborhood, then two more, then three more. They were followed by college students walking in pairs. By the time we all got downtown and joined people coming from the west, north and south, I felt like I was back in New York, walking out of Grand Central Station, except I didn't have to step over anyone sleeping on the sidewalk in broad daylight.

Rick had turned Grand Rapids into an art gallery two years before, but this was on a much grander scale. There was art everywhere you looked. Six city neighborhoods contained a total of 164 different venues. Art was found inside museums, boutiques, coffee shops, restaurants, banks, vacant buildings, and city parks. There was so much art that downtown Grand Rapids couldn't hold it all. Finding it was like going on an incredible Easter egg hunt complete with maps and smart phone GPS assistance. We had never seen anything even close to this in Grand Rapids.

Mass transit in the form of RAPID buses was the order of the day. Either that or you had to park and walk. The roads were too jammed to drive. Parking lots were overflowing.

The success of ArtPrize 2011 was almost impossible to measure the traditional way because just as it was totally open to the arts community, there were no barriers at all to the public. It was totally free. No one paid admission. There were no gates to go into or out of. There was no way to measure the crowd size or what they were spending.

As far as the way event management was usually done, this was total anarchy. But it totally worked, as documented by Anderson Economic Group, LLC for Experience, the Grand Rapids Convention and Visitors Bureau, following ArtPrize 2011.

The AEG study found more than 213,000 adults and children attended ArtPrize 2011 and they came with cash and credit cards, spending more than $10.1 million, extrapolating that out to show a net economic impact of $15.4 million.

The event also brought 1,582 artists from 36 countries and 42 states to Grand Rapids at 164 different venues. That is part of the intangible ArtPrize benefits according to the AEG report. It also points out that 100 schools and more than 7,700 students were in downtown Grand Rapids for ArtPrize as the result of the program "ARTcation," along with student field trips and an early childhood program.

"These children had the chance to see the city and consider art work they otherwise may not have been exposed to," wrote the study's authors Scott D. Watkins and Tyler M. Theile. Perhaps most importantly they wrote, "This type of educational experience plants a seed for the next generation of creative people in the community."

ArtPrize 2011 also contributed to the reinvention of this American community in a very concrete way. The study points out the people who owned the sites of more than 160 venues and eight information hubs "completed property improvement and beautification projects that provide long-term quality benefits to the area."

Some people said the day after; they were slightly disappointed that with ArtPrize, Grand Rapids still seemed to be preaching to the choir. For the most part, people who came to ArtPrize were from West Michigan. In fact, most were from metro Grand Rapids. However, it should not be assumed those people were all that familiar with downtown and how it had been reinvented.

The AEG study shows 98 percent of people who responded to the survey's questionnaires said they were just as likely, or more likely, to visit Grand Rapids within a year after ArtPrize.

What really made an impact was the presence of 25 media outlets at ArtPrize. Grand Rapids got good media coverage—no, Grand Rapids got great press – in USA Today, The New York Times, The Detroit News, and The Washington Post, along with most of the major TV network and cable TV news shows.

ArtPrize 2009 through 2011 and what I like to call the "Bliss Factor" gave us a real education in several things. To begin with they demonstrated that social media is the 800-pound gorilla that you want on your side. This beast should be your best friend. If it turns on you, you need to react quickly and you need to not fight fire with fire, but social media with social media.

That is a wonderful lesson to learn for the next cluster of prosperity.

Don't be afraid to shine your light to the world, and don't be afraid of using innovative ways to do it.

The fact that Grand Rapids City Hall invited Bliss into its fold contains so many lessons for that next cluster. However the "celebrate diversity" umbrella seems to cover it all

And finally, there is nothing wrong with reinforcing community pride. It is amazing what can happen when you invited everyone into your tent and give them real ownership in your vision. That is partnership.

CHAPTER TWENTY-ONE:
The Decade That Made the Difference

WHAT A DIFFERENCE a decade can make. In 2002, Richard Florida ranked Grand Rapids as 38th among 49 cities in his "Gay Friendly Index." Ten years later, Grand Rapids was outed by Advocate.com, as one of the ten, "Gayest Cities in America."

"The heart of western Michigan LGBT life is in Grand Rapids, with dancing, drinking, and bingo at the Apartment (ApartmentLounge.net), which has been in operation for over three decades; karaoke at Diversions video bar (DiversionsNightclub.com), and drag shows and go-go boys at Rumors (RumorsNightclub.net). The city boasts one of the Midwest's best LGBT country line-dancing scenes, with the Grand River Renegades (GrandRiverRenegades.com) offering anyone a dance card on Sundays at Rumors."[26]

This is not the Grand Rapids I moved into in 1990.

As the auto industry is re-born in Detroit, Grand Rapids has given birth to the Medical Mile and could become a life sciences hub perhaps for the world, maybe for the nation, but most certainly for Michigan.

Medical Mile has already had a huge impact on Grand Rapids. If nothing else, it turned a blue-collar, sleepy, locked-in-the-past neighborhood on the northeast side of the city into one of the shooting stars in Michigan.

The evidence of that can be seen in real estate values. The site of a Burger King on Michigan Street was sold for $5.6 million as construction on Medical Mile began. Close to ten years later, The Grand Rapids Press building was sold to Michigan State University for $12 million.

Medical Mile has also grown upon itself. A second tier of health care

---

26   Matthew Breen, "Gayest Cities in America, 2012" *Advocate.com* , Jan. 9, 2012. Accessed February 4, 2012

has been built upon the foundation built by Spectrum Health, Van Andel Institute, Grand Valley State University and Michigan State University. Specialists are starting to nest in new construction like Women's Health Center and Midtown Surgical Center.

"We are going to see more of that," said Alliance for Health President Lody Zwarensteyn. "Specialists like to be near their bases of operation, which in many cases will be the hospitals."

The development of the Mile has also driven change on Monroe Center, the business and retail hub of downtown Grand Rapids. Twelve years after Steketee's Department Store moved out of its flagship store on that street in 1998, Michigan Blue Cross Blue Shield moved in. This is definitely Medical Mile and health care industry related. However the Blues relocation from the suburbs to the city was more than that because of what it was replacing

The eight-story, 108,000-square foot retail giant that was built in 1915 became not a symbol of Grand Rapids' past, but of Grand Rapids' frustration in the present, and worries for the future.

The Steketee's building was destined to become another example of the Grand Rapids community reinventing itself. Rockford Construction, led by John Wheeler, a man who has yet to lose his pony tail and his love of Harley-Davidson motorcycles, took the lead on the Steketee's project.

With backing from those who had money in Grand Rapids, especially Peter Secchia; Wheeler combined the three separate buildings that made up the Steketee's flagship footprint into a single building.

Finding new tenants for this monster was not easy. But finally it was announced that the Blues would re-locate.

When the insurance company decided to move from the suburbs back to downtown Grand Rapids it was cause for a celebration. That building is now home not only to the Blues but to Schuler Books & Music and a branch of Independent Bank. However, the Blues came first.

"We are not a retail downtown, we are a services downtown. And, a lot of those services are health care," said Lody.

It also should be noted that Schuler Books & Music is in that building because the community's leaders decided Grand Rapids had to have a downtown book store. Several had tried. All had failed. The community made sure this one stayed.

And so the reinvention of this American community continues.

Michigan Street Corridor, the neighborhood that surrounds the concrete artery that woke up to find it was the Medical Mile, is also about to be reinvented with the help of Grand Rapids city leaders. They are offering the 50,000 people who live and work there the opportunity to help them design a new, more livable, more sustainable neighborhood.

If one benchmark of its success is the reinvention of Grand Rapids, the answer is unequivocally, yes. The Medical Mile has worked.

But, will it become a magnet for health care and life sciences research regionally, nationally or even globally?

While it may not be a Medical Mecca yet, the Mile has served as a great attractor of medical talent. I see it on Michigan Street NE whenever I take the mile-and-a-half walk from my home to the center of downtown. What a difference a decade made. This street that was empty now vibrates with the movement of students, teachers, doctors, nurses and all of the allied health professionals streaming in and out of Spectrum-Butterworth downtown at shift change, seven days a week, 24 hours a day.

Here's a key lesson to be learned for the next cluster of prosperity. The cluster should not operate in a vacuum. This reinvention is not only happening on Michigan Street. I can see it on the Saint Mary's downtown campus, and in Metro Health Village, where a new community was invented.

Why is this happening? This talent is being attracted to metro Grand Rapids by opportunity.

"There is a musical chairs game going on among a lot of the staff," explained Zwarensteyn. "A nurse can work at your place today, a different place tomorrow and another place the day after."

It is more than that. It is also the opportunity to practice medicine, do research, and teach a class all on Michigan Street NE, or by taking a walk down to Saint Mary's or a short drive to Metro in Wyoming.

It is not just happening in Grand Rapids. This is not a silo. We are seeing this all along the state's life sciences corridor, from Detroit to Ann Arbor to Grand Rapids to Kalamazoo.

The Business Leaders for Michigan (BLM) 2012 Michigan Turnaround Plan shows that Michigan universities were responsible for the eighth highest number of university bio-science degrees in the nation and the state is 15th in employment in that industry sector.

Of course, Medical Mile claims only a portion of those numbers. Yet, it is still a key component in the state's life sciences sector that the BLM plan points to as one of the six drivers of the new economy in Michigan.

The state's research universities are sixth in the nation in terms of R&D expenditure per student and Michigan registers more 20-percent more patents than the U.S. average.

The BLM Turnaround Plan authors wrote, that there is "an existing industry to build on," with more than 20-thousand people employed directly in bio-pharma in Michigan and another 75-thousand in related industries in 2008."

We also have the advantage of lessons learned in the transformation of Michigan Street NE into the Medical Mile. And we have seen a new generation of entrepreneurs born in Grand Rapids along with that reinvention.

We have also learned we need more than brains. We need resolve. We need courage. We have to take a risk.

Look at Detroit and what happened there. Locked into a post-World War Two industrial, parochial mentality, the Motor City stalled and took Michigan down with it. We have learned that no city, no state, can be a company town anymore. Celebrate the diversity.

Put this down as another lesson learned from the Medical Mile experience that will be useful when we do this again, and rest assured, we are going to have to do this again. We can't turn Medical Mile into Grand Rapids' version of Detroit's Big Three.

"It's going to plateau. It's going to do its thing and it will be a key part of our economy. But it will not be the growth part of our economy," said VAI's Jerry Callahan. "That is going to come from many growth sectors, life science being one of them."

Even if we don't have a drastic restructuring ahead of us, sectors like life sciences and advanced manufacturing have to grow and evolve. We have to do much more than simply not stand in the way.

The Right Place Inc. President Birgit Klohs believes the Grand Rapids and West Michigan of the future will be a very robust community with a diverse business base. She foresees a community that is not dependent on any one industry.

"What that also requires is for the citizens of West Michigan to embrace the world in all of its shades and opinions. We have to understand that our (private sector) companies will be coming from different parts of the world and that enriches us."

One of the strongest lessons learned is that Grand Rapids has to be more inclusive and more welcoming. Standing tall with arms crossed is not a welcoming gesture. We have to keep our arms open, to truly welcome people who speak differently, who eat different foods, worship different gods or perhaps don't worship any God at all.

"We need to make a mental shift to become a more sophisticated, accepting community," she said. "Talent doesn't just want an infrastructure in which they do their research. Talent also needs nurturing when they leave the research bench. They need to find a community that has the arts, a community that also allows for different thought processes."

Another transferable lesson learned is that we can no longer expect that our children are going to stay close to home. Just as the world is invited into Grand Rapids now, our young people are being invited and enticed to move far away and stay away.

Alex Gilde and Dr. Sarah Mattson, an MSU College of Human Medicine student and an MSU graduate, respectively, whom we met a few chapters ago, are staying in West Michigan. They are homeowners in the Grand Rapids area. They like it here. But will those who follow them make the same decision?

Rich West is another life science player we met earlier who has decided to stay, making his home in Coopersville and creating his dreams on four feet of lab bench space in Kalamazoo's Southwest Michigan Innovation Center. But he too is worried about those who come after him, the fresh minds who might decide West Michigan isn't good enough.

"I hate to say it, but Michigan is one of the top exporters of college graduates and that breaks my heart," he told me the day we met in Coopersville. "There are a lot of smart people here with a great work ethic. But they are leaving."

We have also learned that we need to prepare the generations that follow us to take Grand Rapids to its next stage. The Medical Mile is not a magic silver bullet.

Another very valuable lesson that will apply to what comes our way in the future is the need to carve out a space for entrepreneurs. The new generation will need spaces like the West Michigan Science and Technology Initiative. The new generation will need a community where talent can flourish. Grand Rapids does not need another version of Silicon Valley. We need another version of this cluster of prosperity, Medical Mile.

Perhaps we will see the next Homer Stryker born inside the Southwest Michigan Innovation Center in Kalamazoo, another excellent home for idea incubation.

"The Innovation Center was built by and for the people who were being displaced by Pfizer. Some people say it was luck," Southwest Michigan First CEO Ron Kitchens told me. "I am a man of faith and believe it was a divine blessing."

Ron also believes the Innovation Center will be serving a different kind of entrepreneur in the years ahead, predicting we are going to see much more of the "passionate inventor" as opposed to the "displaced scientist."

We have also learned that Medical Mile is not a straight line. Partnerships are being built along the way taking it far from the Mile's home base of Michigan Street NE.

Many of the Innovation Center's tenants are using equipment that was donated by Van Andel Institute. There we have evidence of another reinvention lesson learned: the value of partnerships even between entities and communities that could see themselves in competition with each other cannot be underestimated.

Van Andel Institute CEO Dave Van Andel knows the value of those partnerships.

"I think one of the gratifying things for me has been the fact that our initial decision to locate the institute in West Michigan has been greeted with several follow-on, independent decisions by other organizations to invest alongside (us), to create the Medical Mile to begin with."

He said that showed, in the early days, there was some momentum and energy behind the idea of creating a medical/scientific powerhouse in West Michigan. As more and more people are attracted to the Mile, Grand Rapids could reach the point where it is ready to compete on a global stage.

Remember this: very few people thought this would work in the beginning. I had a chance to talk to one of the people who were with Dave at the beginning. She remembers working out of boxes and being told time and time again that Grand Rapids was exactly the wrong place to do something like the VAI. And don't even ask what people were saying about the Medical Mile.

The reinvention of Grand Rapids proved them all wrong.

"And, when you can do that, you know what? West Michigan will have an opportunity to become a destination site for not just science, but for health care, for breakthroughs in the development in new drugs, new therapies and new devices and West Michigan becomes in its own right, and maybe Michigan in time, the third angle in the triangle between Boston and the Bay area," said Van Andel.

"It doesn't replace anything but it will add a significant new dimension to what is already here."

We have also learned that the way we finance our future has to change. We have to allow more people to contribute. We need to do more than just "allow." We have to devise new ways to "invite" them to contribute because business always goes where it is invited. We also have to remember that "profit" can work in tandem with "philanthropy."

The investment model in Grand Rapids has changed because of Medical Mile. It is moving from one of philanthropy to one of capitalism. Outside money is being welcomed. Smaller investors are being sought. However, there remains what The Charter Group VP Dale Grogan described as "an investment gap" that has to be closed.

This is not a strictly West Michigan phenomenon. It is happening worldwide, driven by people who believe they are doing more than starting new businesses. They are fueling social and community change.

And this is not just a case of transformational U.S. capitalism. It is happening in Great Britain, The Netherlands and Hong Kong. In fact, they are far ahead of us.

To continue this momentum in the United States, we are going to have to see some reform at the federal level like the bi-partisan legislative effort to allow more of us to take part in this new investment model at street level to open the investment doors to the $25-thousand or even $250 investor.

The Jumpstart Our Business Startups (JOBS) Act that was signed by President Obama in April 2012 is intended to be a move in that direction. It includes a crowdfunding provision that allows companies to raise money from unaccredited individual investors through a broker or an online funding platform. A $1 million cap would be put on the money raised by any one entrepreneur or startup organization.

This provision also allows companies to reach a higher threshold before they have to go public with their expansion plans. Facebook COO Sheryl Sandberg told POLITICO that would have allowed her company to remain private, instead of raising money through an IPO.[27] That was a mess that could have been avoided. Critics of the JOBS Act though are pointing to the Facebook IPO fiasco as proof that retail investors need more protection.[28]

We have also learned the value of a public-private partnership in which one side cannot be successful without the other.

Grand Rapids owes the Van Andel and DeVos families a debt of

---

27   Michelle Quinn and Jonathan Allen, "Facebook: JOBS Act would have affected IPO" *Politico.com*, April 6, 2012. Accessed April 7, 2012.

28   Jess Kamen, "Facebook reignites JOBS Act debate," *Politico.com*, May 24, 2012. Accessed May 27, 2012

gratitude for the money, time, energy and sweat they have poured into the city and the community. They did much more than simply write checks.

But they did not do it alone. The public sector's role cannot be forgotten, nor can it be minimized for the future.

Jay Van Andel did donate $1 billion for the Van Andel Institute. However, Gov. John Engler committed $1 billion of Michigan's money from the state's share of the tobacco settlement fund in 1999 to help build the state's Life Sciences Corridor from Detroit to Grand Rapids.

When Pfizer Corp. bought out Pharmacia and jobs were threatened in Kalamazoo and Holland, Gov. Jennifer Granholm put together a $635 million tax incentive proposal in a failed effort to convince Pfizer to keep the Pharmacia buildings and the people inside them working at full capacity.

That didn't work. Granholm still had West Michigan's back. She presented a ceremonial check for $10 million for a new Biosciences Research and Commercialization Center in Kalamazoo. That was part of the effort to keep ex-Pfizer scientists, researchers and technicians in West Michigan by offering them a chance to create their own businesses.

One year later, in 2004, the Granholm administration committed $2.3 million in MEDC and Core Communities Fund money to the Grand Rapids Smart Zone, the fifth-floor of the Cook-DeVos Center for Health Sciences, the home of the West Michigan Science and Technology Initiative.

That stream of funding continued with a $500,000 MEDC grant awarded to WMSTI at the end of 2011. But state government's involvement is at a much smaller scale thanks to Michigan's beleaguered economy along with a Governor (Rick Snyder) and a Republican-led legislature that don't see the wisdom in investing in a government-innovation partnership.

Financial conservatives on Capitol Hill and in Lansing have been saying for years that "governments should not be picking winner and losers." Isn't that what leadership is all about, deciding which direction we should be going and showing us the way?

During our conversation in his office, Dave Van Andel told me that part of the challenge facing Medical Mile and Van Andel Institute has been an ongoing one. "The state (of Michigan) has to decide whether it is in or out. And it has to stop this start and stop, stop and start, stop, start, stop. There has to be some consistency to its thought process."

The Life Science Corridor concept that began in Gov. John Engler's administration, had a 20-year horizon with allocations of $50 million a year, "and away we went," Van Andel said. "We never hit that 20-year mark.

We never did all of the things we wanted to do. Today, I don't think there is even $5 million allocated to this."

Besides the funding issue, Dave also wants to see some regulatory issues addressed to make Michigan more competitive in this arena.

"These are things that can be fixed and my hope is now with a new 'organization' in Lansing and with a new Governor (Snyder) that they will see the importance of that and bring some consistency back."

"I would not necessarily agree with that," said Ron Kitchens. "Health sciences, life sciences, have to be competitive. Pfizer is not funding research projects long-term. They are funding things as you hit benchmarks."

He argued that the best companies are creating funding chaos on purpose because they believe that it "accelerates and forces cream to the top, and it forces people to be efficient and effective."

Ron would like to see more federal research dollars pushed more toward small companies and less to academia. He also admitted that is a double-edged sword. It could create the unintended consequence of giving those institutions that do become more entrepreneurial and private sector-driven an advantage in the free market.

We have learned the value of debate, haven't we? But we also know how to compromise for the common good.

We have learned the value of a shared vision. And perhaps this is the greatest lesson of all. This could be that magic silver bullet that economic developers are always in search of.

Jerry Callahan told me that in in 10 years he believes we will begin to see a good portion of economic development happening around Medical Mile now "starting to gain traction, starting to create that fertile ground."

Five years after that, Callahan believes we will begin to see Medical Mile as a real idea magnet, "attracting significant ideas from the hinterlands. We won't have to fight for them. They will come to us for funding and leadership"

And then in 20 years, Callahan predicts we will see the major players in the bio-and medical-technology space moving to Grand Rapids. That would mean major corporations are re-locating here, bringing with them thousands of employees, all because they want to be part of this Medical Mile energy.

But through all the conversations, email exchanges and research that went into this book I think Callahan said it best when he told me, "This is an all boats rising situation and we have to keep reminding ourselves of that."

There we have the greatest lesson from the reinvention of this American community. We have to see ourselves as a player on the world stage, no longer parochial and isolated, but a village in the global community.

This goes beyond the lives saved, the hearts transplanted, the babies birthed and the businesses yet to born. This shared, global vision is our foundation for the future that has been built on Michigan Street NE. That is what this is really all about. This is what will give us our new sense of place.

As Jerry Callahan told me, "Our vision has to be greater than a 13-county area. We have to realize Medical Mile is not a straight line. It is a concentric circle that goes around the world."

What do you want to do next?

Afterword

THIS PUBLIC-PRIVATE-PHILANTHROPIC SECTOR PARTNERSHIP that has reinvented Grand Rapids has been a wonderful thing to behold. All sides working together, all sides buying in, even when there are some weeks that it doesn't work so well. Yet, it is working.

What do we want to do next?

We have a long list of options from which to choose in Grand Rapids. If there is one thing this community has always been good at, it is the creation of clusters of prosperity. Some work better than others as I have attempted to show in *Last Chance Mile: The Reinvention of an American Community*. However I believe that there is one cluster of prosperity that is coming back to life, a cluster with a stronger chance of succeeding than any other in West Michigan, and this could be true for your community too.

Manufacturing.

Manufacturing matters. That point was driven home in June 2012 when the U.S. Department of Commerce Bureau of Economic Analysis reported that "durable-goods manufacturing was the largest contributor to U.S. real GDP by state growth in 2011. This industry increased 7.9 percent in 2011, after increasing 17.0 percent in 2010. It was the leading contributor to real GDP growth in six of the eight BEA regions and in 26 states. Durable-goods manufacturing contributed 3.94 percentage points to growth in Oregon and 1.17 percentage points to growth in Michigan.

Professional, scientific, and technical services and information services were also leading contributors to U.S. real GDP by state growth. Professional, scientific, and technical services increased 4.9 percent in 2011, matching its 2010 growth rate."

The death of manufacturing has been greatly exaggerated in Michigan, as Mark Twain might have said. Manufacturing has also been greatly disparaged. While Wall Street and Main Street were buying into the hysteria of the dot-com bubble and even while Medical Mile was being built, manufacturing was pushed to the sidelines. It waited on the bench like a major league baseball player, chewing his tobacco, spitting, doing everything he could to help the team, but still muttering, "Put me in, coach. Put me in."

It is time to put him in, Coach. Manufacturing never went away. He was always there, sometimes on the bench, sometimes in the field, doing what had to be done, just waiting for another chance. That time is now.

Manufacturing made Michigan. Detroit, Flint, Saginaw, Kalamazoo, Jackson, Benton Harbor, St. Joseph and Grand Rapids all hummed to the vibrations of the auto, furniture, military, appliance and aerospace industries. They still do albeit to a lesser extent than we saw in the 20th century.

We are still very good at thinking of things and making things. Or to paraphrase Thomas Edison, we figure out what the world needs and then we start inventing. He was from Michigan, by the way, a good friend of Henry Ford and you know his story.

After a decade in Hell, the factories are starting to hum again. General Motors, Ford, and Chrysler had one of their best sales months in years in May 2012. Reshoring, manufacturing that is moving back to the U.S. from China and Mexico, is having an impact.

Harry Moser, founder and president of Reshoring Initiative told me we have the "500-pound gorilla in the room" to thank for that, China.

"Wages (in China) are going up 20-to-25 percent per year, while ours are only going up 2-to-3-percent," said Moser. "So you have a rapid compression of cost."

He believes that trend is going to continue because of China's one-child-one-family population control policy.

"China's labor shortage is bad now and it is only going to get worse because of that policy that was put into place 30 years ago," said Moser.

That is the kind of forecast that GR Spring & Stamping CEO Jim Zawacki does, and doesn't, want to hear. Reshoring carries with it a bittersweet flavor. The work coming back to the U.S. is putting a new strain on the manufacturers who are seeing orders doubling and even tripling overnight.

Zawacki told me that "increased business used to be a great thing. Now it is a capacity issue for everyone. You have to say 'uncle' at some point."

However that does not mean Zawacki sees the increase in business as a bad thing. It just means that manufacturers, like him, are being faced with a new set of management decisions.

There isn't a single manufacturer I spoke with in the first half of 2012 whose business was not improving to the point of "doing very well." That carried with it the problem of finding enough talent to handle the increased production. They were all inventing new ways to do the business they had been doing in some cases for generations.

One West Michigan community, Kentwood, has dealt with more than $20 million in requests for manufacturing tax breaks in the first half of 2012 because of plant expansions and equipment improvements. Many of them are directly related to the auto industry supply chain.

Manufacturing in West Michigan is impacted by Medical Mile. Take for example a joint venture manufacturing partnership that stretches from Middleville to Holland and to Zeeland. This new partnership is happening because of the networking formed on Grand Rapids' Michigan Street NE.

It is the classic case of one company, LumenFlow Corp. in Middleville, having a great idea and finding a partner, Venntis Technology LLC in Holland that could make it happen. They were brought together by a third party, an organization that is all about helping move new ideas to market, West Michigan Science and Technology Initiative (WMSTI) and the West Michigan Medical Device Consortium (WWMDC), both of which call the GVSU Cook-DeVos Center for Health Sciences home both of which we were introduced in previous chapters.

LumenFlow and Venntis Technologies have formed "United Lumen" to develop patent-pending high-efficiency LED Light Engine designs that all parties told me will surpass anything on the market and make all of us much more comfortable with LED technology to light our homes and offices.

Here is one more example of innovative medical device manufacturing in West Michigan. This one is really not associated with Medical Mile. Yet it is a case of a business doing its business in a different fashion, forming partnerships, and especially in this case, inviting business to come its way. Asking for ideas, accepting those ideas, and making dreams come true for people who suddenly have a voice.

This collaborative spirit, this process of moving from individual to collective insight, resulting in "praxis," the practical application of knowledge, is not limited to Grand Rapids' Medical Mile.

The medical device industry could be one of West Michigan's most under-appreciated sectors. This is worth repeating. "Once you lift the cover you will be surprised what's there," said MarketLab Inc.'s new product development manager, Tom Howing.

He came down the hall of the MarketLab complex in Caledonia for our meeting, a little out of breath, a little flushed in the face and carrying two bottles of water. Howing is a man on a mission.

Howing, who is also a member of the West Michigan Medical Device Consortium Task Force, told me, "It is kind of a personal mission of mine to say 'how can I make an impact in the community?'"

MarketLab's mission, according to company literature is to be "the leading direct mail catalog supplier of specialty products and services for healthcare professionals in North America." However they are also, as Howing's job title would imply, creating and taking new products to market.

"It (product development) really starts with our customers, going out and listening to them, understanding what they need, and then working with our partners," MarketLab President Steve Bosio told me.

Market Lab's Spark program is moving the company beyond listening to the people who are working in the operating, examination and emergency rooms of those customers. "Spark" is designed to rake innovation from around the medical community into a system for development and marketing.

This is a portal for new ideas. It doesn't even have to be a health care idea. "We vet it and see if it is marketable. If it does look viable, we will manufacture it or find someone who can," Howing explained. "And there is no risk to the person who had the idea."

This new model for the reinvention of an American community is working.

What is the thread that binds this quilt together? Howing put it best when he told me, "Most of what we get is medical, but I have received a plan to build a better mousetrap," Howing said. "The entrepreneurial spirit is alive and well.

As I said, it is going to take more than just one cluster of prosperity to truly reinvent this American community, Grand Rapids, Mich. When it comes to clusters there is no reason to limit the possibilities. The list of business clusters on The Right Place Inc. website is lengthy, to say the least. It runs from automotive to biopharmaceuticals to prefabricated enclosures to tobacco. Heavy machinery, metal manufacturing, aerospace engines, and agricultural products are also on the list of more than 20 business clusters that I would call, clusters of prosperity.

So manufacturers are working together and forming new partnerships just as the scientists, technicians, physicians, surgeons, students, teachers and entrepreneurs are doing on Medical Mile.

Manufacturing is back. As Zawacki said, that is opening the door to a new set of problems, or at least a set of problems that we have not seen in decades. One of the biggest is the lack of skilled workers for these 21ˢᵗ century factories. How did that happen? One manufacturer in Grand Rapids told me that we "skipped a generation."

However, we can fix that. Education will be as big a part of this developing cluster of prosperity as it has been to the Medical Mile cluster.

What Grand Rapids has been good at through history is the ability to be a community in flux. This American community has been able to adapt and morph, like a chameleon, when change is needed for survival. When a new model is needed, a new model is built.

The pieces are already here. Again, this is like doing a crossword puzzle. You never start with 1A. You find something that you can do. You do it well, and then you move on from there.

The list is constantly being reinvented. New clusters of prosperity are being added. The Right Place Inc. has identified food processing as one of the growing clusters of prosperity in West Michigan. State of Michigan economic development officials agree. In fact, they believe the clusters of agriculture and manufacturing actually overlap and see a real synergy among almost all of the clusters of prosperity in Michigan.

You might be surprised by this. I was. One of the strongest of Grand Rapids' clusters of prosperity is entertainment. I didn't think much of that until a friend in the Detroit area told me about the weekend he and his partner had spent in this American community on the banks of the Grand River.

He had never been to Grand Rapids as a tourist and was amazed to see how many restaurants were in the downtown district. "When you see that, you know something is happening," he explained pointing his finger and raising his 72 year old eyebrows for emphasis.

He's right. There is something happening in Grand Rapids, Mich. In fact, there is a lot happening in this American community. The same could be true for your American community. It all begins with a shared vision.

SOME FINAL NOTES

VAN ANDEL RESEARCH INSTITUTE, Michigan State University College of Human Medicine, Spectrum Health Systems, West Michigan Science and Technology Initiative, Metro Health, Kent Intermediate School District, and Grand Valley State University have been very approachable, open and helpful in putting this book together.

If you ever have an opportunity to tour the facilities of Medical Mile or meet the people involved, I would encourage you to do that. I am confident their attitude toward you will be no different than it was toward me.

I would also like to encourage you to contact me with any questions or comments. If you are working on building a cluster of prosperity in your American community, I would love to hear about it.

Until we meet again, I think you will find these books worth reading.

Images of America: Grand Rapids Furniture City by Norma Lewis, Arcadia Publishing. This book has some incredible photos of the people of the Grand Rapids furniture industry from the "Early Days" through "The Transition," when as Lewis writes, "In the end, neither strikes nor natural disasters defeated the Grand Rapids home furnishings industry. North Carolina did."

Transplanting the Passion, by Michael Lezon and John Leegwater, Metro Health Hospital. The authors of this book do a great job of telling the history of Metro Health, beginning with the group of osteopathic doctors who pooled their money to build the first hospital of osteopathic medicine in Grand Rapids.

Heart & Soul, The Story of Grand Rapids Neighborhoods by Linda Samuelson, Wm. B Eerdmans Publishing Co. Linda Samuelson, a former Grand Rapids city commission put together a wonderful book telling the stories of Grand Rapids diverse neighborhoods.

The Story of Grand Rapids, edited by Z.Z. Lydens, Kregel Publications. Lydens is considering to be one of the two leading historians of the city of Grand Rapids. I relied heavily on this book and was constantly amazed by the detail to which this former newspaper reporter and editor goes into telling the story of this American community.

Grand Rapids: A City Renewed by Gordon L. Olson, Grand Rapids Historical Commission. Olson is considered to be the preeminent historian in the city of Grand Rapids because of his series of books that tell the story of The Furniture City.

The Oxford History of the American People, by Samuel Eliot Morrison, Oxford University Press. This book tells the story of Grand Rapids in the very early years as only someone of that time period can tell it.

Michigan: A Guide to the Wolverine State, Oxford University Press. This is an incredibly interesting book written during the Great Depression by writers put to work through the WPA. They are described as "hungry, writers who cinched up their belts and with stubby pencils went to work" chronicling the history of the U.S., state by state.

Strike: How the Furniture Workers Strike of 1911 Changed Grand Rapids by Jeffrey Kleiman, Wayne State University Press. This book will really open your eyes about the relationship between the titans of industry in Grand Rapids and the people who worked for them. That is all I am going to write now. Please read this.

Reinventing Discovery: The New Era of Networked Science, by Michael Nielsen, Princeton University Press. This book has absolutely nothing to do with Grand Rapids' Medical Mile and it has absolutely everything to do with Medical Mile. You really must read this to understand how networked science grows upon itself and how that model can be used inside and outside clusters of prosperity.

Back To Work, Why We Need Smart Government for a Strong Economy by Bill Clinton, Knopf. This book is inspirational. Before you even think about creating a cluster of prosperity in your American community, read this book. And before you start trashing the role of government in America, read this book.

Talk to you soon,

Rod

*West Michigan was shocked to learn hearts were being transplanted
inside Spectrum Health's Meijer Heart Center.*

*Spectrum-Butterworth Hospital is one of the anchor institutions of
Grand Rapids' Medical Mile. It is also the flagship of West Michigan's
largest health care organization, Spectrum Health Systems Inc.*

Helen DeVos Children's Hospital is the tallest building on Medical Mile and is one of the tallest buildings in Grand Rapids. However, as impressive as the structure is, it pales in comparison with what is going on inside the hospital.

Medical Mile began with the creation of Van Andel Research Institute where scientists from around the world are working on curing cancer, Alzheimer's, Parkinson's disease and a number of other illnesses that are plaguing the world.

Van Andel Research Institute is wrapped almost protectively around Medical Mile's link to the 19th century, Immanuel Lutheran Church.

Dr. Craig Webb is one of the Medical Mile pioneers.

Rick DeVos created ArtPrize, a non-juried international art show that took Grand Rapids by storm. He is also leading a drive to launch more entrepreneurs in West Michigan.

Rich DeVos and Jay Van Andel's first business venture was a flight school. Although that didn't work out, they went on to create Amway and become billionaires.

Doug DeVos and Steve Van Andel in front of portraits of their fathers are taking Amway into the 21st century guided by the foundations laid out by their Rich DeVos and Jay Van Andel.

Gov. John Engler signed the legislation that created the Life Sciences Corridor with Dave Van Andel looking on (far left).